BY THE GRACE OF G-D

KALEIDOSCOPE
UPLIFTING VIEWS ON DAILY LIFE

*From the life and teachings of the Rebbe
Rabbi Menachem Mendel Schneerson
of righteous memory*

Compiled and adapted by
Dovid Zaklikowski

HASIDIC
archives

Kaleidoscope © 2017 Hasidic Archives
www.HasidicArchives.com
HasidicArchives@gmail.com
Facebook.com/HasidicArchives

ISBN 978-1-944875-02-2
Design by Design is Yummy and
Hasidic Archives Studios
Printed in Malaysia

For my children
Motti, Meir, Shaina,
Benny and Mendel

The Rebbe, Rabbi Menachem Mendel Schneerson

CONTENTS

Introduction	1		Food	53
Action	3		Gathering	55
Anti-Semitism	7		Harmony	57
Apology	9		Holidays	59
Birthdays	11		Humility	63
Books	13		Illustrations	65
Calling	15		Intellect	67
Caution	17		Joy	69
Chabad House	19		Justice	71
Challenges	21		Kindness	73
Charity	25		Language	75
Charity Box	27		Leadership	77
Childhood	29		Light	81
Conflict	28		Livelihood	83
Clubs	31		Maimonides	85
Conflict	33		Matter	87
Darkness	35		Mentor	89
Days	37		Mergers	91
Differences	39		Mitzvah	93
Drugs	43		Morality	97
Education	45		Moshiach	99
Elderly	47		Neighbors	101
Extrovert	49		Obstacles	103
Femininity	51		Outreach	105

Parents	109
Peace	111
Peer Pressure	113
Prayer	115
Prevention	117
Pride	119
Priorities	121
Prison	123
Protection	125
Purpose	127
Racism	129
Rebuilding	131
Rebuke	133
Redemption	135
Repentance	139
Respect	141
Responsibility	143
Retirement	145
Self-Motivation	149
Sight	151
Speech	153
Song	155
Teaching	157
Technology	159
Terror	161
Unity	163
Uplift	165
Wealth	167
Women	171
The Rebbe	175
Glossary	199
Sources	202
Acknowledgements	207

INTRODUCTION

Known simply as the Rebbe, Rabbi Menachem Mendel Schneerson inspired a generation of men and women to revive Jewish observance around the world. Until this day, his teachings are studied by Chabad followers, admirers, and laymen who simply enjoy the Rebbe's novel approach to Torah.

In a 1960 interview, William Frankel, editor of the *Jewish Chronicle*, asked the Rebbe to address current events in America, Israel and Britain, which he did with ease. Surprised, Mr. Frankel asked how the Rebbe was able to respond so quickly to complex questions. "Why not?" the Rebbe answered. "There are no new problems. In the long history of the Jewish people, there have been all kinds of problems, and no matter what we have to face, we can find a parallel and the answer in our history."

The Rebbe applied Torah's values and ideals to modern life in a way that made Judaism relevant and vital for a new generation. His long talks delved into biblical stories and complex texts of Jewish law with the same keen interest. Often he began with a well-known concept, and by questioning its premise or drawing an unexpected connection, revealed a hidden meaning and a potent lesson for daily life. To his listeners, learning from the Rebbe was like looking through a kaleidoscope. Each small turn brought a new pattern into view—vivid, intricate and radiating light.

This booklet is a collection of the Rebbe's ideas, adapted from talks, correspondence and first-hand encounters. It is intended to offer only a brief taste of the Rebbe's worldview on each subject. But even in this abridged format, a theme quickly emerges.

The Rebbe viewed this world as a good and holy place. He believed that people are essentially decent, and that every individual matters. He saw people's negativity as superficial, an outer layer hiding their core of goodness. It is my hope that *Kaleidoscope* will help its readers to see the world through the Rebbe's eyes.

Dovid Zaklikowski

ACTION

One of the expressions the Rebbe quoted most often was "The deed is the essential thing." This line from *Ethics of Our Fathers* means that the purpose of Torah study is the good deeds— mitzvahs—that it leads to. The Rebbe delivered many long, scholarly discourses, but they always ended with a practical lesson for daily life. When people told the Rebbe about events they had organized or encounters they had, he invariably asked, "What was the actual result?" He took this approach to a new level in explaining a puzzling passage in Genesis (45:14), in which Joseph and Benjamin cry on each other's shoulders. The Talmud states that each was crying about a calamity which they saw with prophetic vision would happen hundreds of years later, in the other's portion of the Land of Israel:

>>>>>>>>>>

Crying does not fix the issue at hand. At most, it makes you feel better. To deal with the issue, you must take action. Why didn't Joseph and Benjamin cry about the destruction that would take place in their own family's land? Why did they cry for the other? The lesson is that if something bad happens to someone else, and you tried to prevent it but were not successful, then you can empathize and cry for him or her. But if something goes wrong in your own life, if there is a "destruction," then crying does not help. In fact, it may have a negative effect, by leading you to believe that no additional action is necessary. The right thing to do is to move on and begin to rebuild.

ANTI-SEMITISM

During the Gulf War in 1991, Saddam Hussein fired Scud missiles into Israeli cities. Around the world, anti-Semitic acts were on the rise, including riots in the Crown Heights community of Brooklyn, New York.

In Poland, too, the Jewish community was on alert. In a letter to the Council for Polish-Jewish Relations, the Rebbe asserted that the Torah provides the antidote to racial conflict:

Mankind began with a single individual: Adam. G-d designed the human race this way so that every person would know that we descend from the same man, who was created in the image of G-d. As such, no human being can claim to be of superior ancestry. Keeping this in mind will help to cultivate feelings of kinship between all people.

A Chabad "roving rabbi" in Namibia during a light moment with locals.

RABBI MENACHEM M. SCHNEERSON
Lubavitch
770 Eastern Parkway
Brooklyn 13, N. Y.

HYacinth 3-9250

By the Gra
21st of Sh
Brooklyn,

Asbury Park, N. J.

Blessing and Greeting:

I received your letter of February
honor of the birth of a daughter t
May G-d grant that you have true y
born grandchild, as well as from all

Your donation was turned over to o
which, as you know, is dedicated t
may it stand your grandchild in go
her parents to a life of Torah, Ch

I want to take this opportunity to
children upon the worthy thing you
departed husband and their father,
lish the new edition of the "Kuntr
etc. As it will be studied by Jew
certainly be a source of great and
soul of the late Mr. M. J. Simon,
book has been published. Needless
Zechus for you and your children.

With prayerful wishes for your suc
in all your affairs,

With blessing

One of tens of thousands of letters the Rebbe wrote.

APOLOGY

At times, the backlog of correspondence
on the Rebbe's desk was huge. After
the most urgent letters, the Rebbe
prioritized those from people who were
not Chabad followers. "My disciples
will understand the delay; others might
feel slighted," he once told his aide
Dr. Nissan Mindel. In the 1980s, the
backlog reached new heights. When
one individual did not receive a prompt
response, he complained to one of the
Rebbe's aides. The Rebbe immediately
wrote to him, "Let me say at once
that your complaints are completely
justified." Adding that he pleaded
"guilty without explanation," he asked
the man's forgiveness. The man was
shocked at the Rebbe's humility and felt
that he should not have complained.
He wrote again, begging the Rebbe's
pardon. The Rebbe responded:

Surely there was never a greater man than Moses, who, when his elder brother Aaron corrected a ruling he had made, admitted that he was right, "and was not ashamed." Rather, when Aaron corrected him, "Moses heard and it pleased him" (Leviticus 10:20).

Rebbetzin Chaya Mushka Schneerson in her wedding gown.

BIRTHDAYS

Rebbetzin Chaya Mushka Schneerson, the Rebbe's wife, led a very private life. Few ever met her, and even many Chabad followers were unaware of the immense support she provided the Rebbe. At her funeral, the Rebbe's raw emotions were palpable. Despite his pain, the Rebbe encouraged others to take to heart his wife's good deeds and to create initiatives in her memory. A month after her passing, on her birthday, the Rebbe began a mass campaign to publicly celebrate one's Jewish birthday with Jewish study, charity, a gathering with friends and positive resolutions:

Every breath we take and everything that happens around us is miraculous. On our birthdays, we take the time to specifically acknowledge the miraculous events around us. As we mark the miracle of our birth, we reflect on the purity with which we came into this world, and we are given an added measure of strength with which to return to our roots.

BOOKS

The Rebbe called on people to invest in "spiritual furniture" for their homes: holy books and Jewish educational texts. While physical furniture should be preserved in its original condition, books, he emphasized, should be used well:

Time should never be wasted. Time ought to be used to gain knowledge. Having Jewish books in your library will always give you an opportunity—whether you wake during the night or have a few minutes by day—to maximize your time.

CALLING

In the early years of his leadership, when the Chabad ethos of outreach was still developing, the Rebbe frequently stressed that every man, woman and child had a responsibility to care for others, materially and spiritually. On the holiday of Sukkot, the Rebbe used the mitzvah of taking the Four Species (palm branch, citron, myrtle and willow) as an analogy for Jewish unity:

Each of the Four Species is very different. One has a good smell and taste; one only smells good; one only has a good taste; and one has neither taste nor smell. Our sages explain that they represent different kinds of Jews. There's one kind of Jew that is learned and does good deeds, one kind that only practices good deeds, another kind that is just learned, and one that has neither quality. Just as there is no way to fulfill the Sukkot commandment without all four plant species, no Jew can be left behind. The same way we bring together palm, citrus, myrtle and willow, all Jews need to unite together to fulfill G–d's will.

CAUTION

Though steadfast in his faith and convictions, in matters of opinion the Rebbe was extremely cautious. He well knew that a passage of Talmud could be explained in multiple ways, and was careful to leave room for other interpretations. On paper, the Rebbe would edit out absolute and superlative words, such as *must*, *impossible* and *very*. Not being overly confident in your opinion, he explained, is a virtue:

Describing G-d's plans, Job says, "Then did He see it, and declare it; He established it, yea, and searched it out" (28:27). Our sages explain that this verse refers to the four-step process from G-d's initial decision until it is carried out. We can learn from this to check and review four times before making a statement. I realized this myself when I made a statement earlier in the week, which when I looked it up turned out to be inaccurate. The explanation I gave last week does not have any basis. The lesson is that one should not rely on memory for oneself, and surely when teaching others.

CHABAD HOUSE

The Rebbe had a vision that Jewish centers would sprout across the globe, with the goal of reaching every Jew, regardless of affiliation. Today these centers are known as Chabad Houses, and number in the thousands. The Rebbe described their mission statement:

They should be centers that spread goodness and kindness as embodied in Jewish teachings. The spirit of the center should be permeated with Chassidic light, vitality and warmth, based on the three loves—love of G-d, love of Torah, and love of our people, Israel—which are ultimately one love. For G-d, His Torah and His people are one.

CHALLENGES

Why is life so difficult? The question crosses many people's minds daily. Couldn't G-d have made this world without so many challenges? Couldn't He have created people with a strong desire to do good, rather than an inclination for evil? Perhaps most troublesome: Why must we toil for our livelihood? The Rebbe explained:

>>>>>>>>>>

It seems to us that we are alone on this planet, struggling to survive. In fact, G‑d simply wants us to work, to earn our keep. The Creator does not want us to eat "bread of shame," a handout we did nothing to deserve. This applies to every area of life. Through work, by moving forward along a straight and just path, we overcome the obstacles that G‑d sets in our way, revealing our hidden strengths in the process.

CHARITY

Judaism views charity as an act that benefits two people: the one who receives and the one who gives. The Hebrew word for charity, *tzedakah*, stems from the word *tzedek*, which means righteousness, implying that it is a righteous act to give. The Rebbe initiated a charity campaign, distributing coins and making charity boxes available at all communal events so that people would never miss an opportunity to give:

G-d grants you money on loan, and trusts that you will use it wisely. When you give charity to one in need, to someone whom you owe nothing, and give more than you think affordable, G-d, who owes you nothing, will increase His charity toward you, and give with an open hand.

CHARITY BOX

A charity box in the home, the Rebbe said, is a constant reminder to be kind to others. He suggested that every child should keep a box in his or her room, always ready to receive a few coins. Tens of thousands of charity boxes were created for this purpose. The Rebbe advised that the boxes be sold with a disclaimer that the owner may give the full box to a cause of his or her choosing, stressing that the benefit of charity lies in the act, not the specific recipient. He explained that the mitzvah of charity applies not just to large donations, but also to just a few coins:

Every time you give to charity, no matter how much, it is a divine act. The more times you give your hard-earned money to a good cause, the more mitzvahs you do. Giving in large amounts is praiseworthy, but there is also an advantage in giving small amounts many times. If you have money to give, do not hold on to it in the hope that you will eventually have a larger sum. Give whatever you have immediately, and when you have more, give again.

CHILDHOOD

The Rebbe compared a child to a young tree. Just as a sapling must be regularly watered, cared for and watched over until it becomes a strong and beautiful tree, so does the child require attention, love and care so that he or she can grow into a healthy human being. Speaking to educators, the Rebbe stressed that every child deserves the same level of devotion:

When it comes to education, we do not look upon the child as the son or daughter of so-and-so. A parent's merits or demerits are irrelevant when it comes to the child. Every child is the creation of G-d, and should be perceived as equally worthy and unique.

CLUBS

The Rebbe felt that directly combating the irreverence of today's youth would be a futile effort. He instead established a Jewish club, Tzivos Hashem, a "spiritual army" that encourages acts of goodness and motivates a child to strengthen his or her Jewish observance:

The original insignia of Tzivos Hashem in 1981.

The club utilizes contests, gatherings and awards, and is designed as a hierarchy, as all armies are, in which a child graduates to higher rankings, the more "missions" he or she completes. This instills a sense of authority, and the notion that children must respect their parents, teachers and the Commander-in-Chief, G-d Almighty.

CONFLICT

Disagreements did not prevent the Rebbe from developing relationships. Though he was famous for the unconditional acceptance and love he showed to all Jews, he was careful never to let this attitude lead to compromises in Jewish observance or belief. In a long correspondence with the acclaimed sculptor Jacques Lipchitz regarding a specific area of Jewish law, the Rebbe explained his approach:

I am not G-d's policeman. Yet I consider it my duty to exert my influence to prevent a Jew from doing something which, in my opinion, is not recommendable. On the other hand, it is my policy to seek out points of agreement rather than disagreement. Since we have reached an impasse in our discussion, I prefer to turn my attention to points of mutual agreement.

Sculptor Jacques Lipchitz at work in his studio.

DARKNESS

In everything he saw, heard or read, the Rebbe sought a lesson for divine service. Once, he related a story in which two friends, seeking to escape the summer heat, enter a dim, cool basement. One tells the other, "Don't worry about the dark; soon it will be bright." The other responds, "You are mistaken. It will always be dark, but we will become accustomed to the dark."

If you know that it is dark, it is easy to turn on the light. If you know that your spiritual life is lacking, it is simple to remedy the problem. Knowing what is wrong is half the cure. But if you've become accustomed to the dark to the point that you don't notice it, then it is very difficult to find the light. A soul in this situation needs assistance from outside.

DAYS

Many of the Rebbe's talks focused on the special qualities of specific dates and seasons on the Jewish calendar. Studying the theme of an upcoming holiday, the significance of the Hebrew month or the lessons of that week's Torah portion, the Rebbe demonstrated, can bring new relevance to our daily lives. But only if we are willing to make the effort of study and contemplation:

Our sages say (Talmud, Avodah Zarah 3a), "Only the one who toils all week can eat on the Sabbath." This applies equally to the spiritual sphere. With proper preparation, one can have truly meaningful days.

DIFFERENCES

When two Chabad students visited Iran in 1979, they planned to lay the groundwork for the opening of a Chabad House there. Instead, the revolution that ripped through the country led them to spearhead an operation that saved thousands of Jewish children. Just as the revolution was coming to a head, they orchestrated a daring escape in which children were airlifted to Italy, and later brought to the United States. Chabad communities cared for the children's physical needs and encouraged them to maintain their unique Persian customs. Chabad helped establish the Persian Jewish Center of Brooklyn, a synagogue and learning center for Iranian families. "The new synagogue and center is certainly a notable achievement...and a source of great rejoicing, not only for the Persian Jewish community, but for all our Jewish people," the Rebbe wrote on the occasion of its opening. To the South African Jewish Board of Deputies, he expressed his appreciation for every community's unique traditions and the importance of preserving them:

> > > > > > > > > >

During the Iranian revolution, children arrive on a Chabad airlift from Iran, 1979.

Virtually every Jewish community comprises a variety of groups, each with a distinct identity in terms of ancestral heritage and traditions, as exemplified by different synagogues with different customs, such as Ashkenazic, Sephardic, Yemenite, etc. Side by side, they contribute to the advancement of the Jewish community as a whole. You surely know that the rabbis in all generations scrupulously upheld the validity of the various canons of prayer services, tracing their diversity to the original twelve tribes of Israel. Experience has shown that whenever a uniform educational system has been imposed on a multifaceted community, it inevitably proves disastrous.

DRUGS

In a private audience with scholar and author Rabbi Adin Even-Yisrael (Steinsaltz), the Rebbe explained that the Torah requires one to be "the master over oneself, and anything that one is enslaved to is wrong." In 1964 the Rebbe wrote that this rule applies with special force to the use of drugs to enhance spiritual experiences:

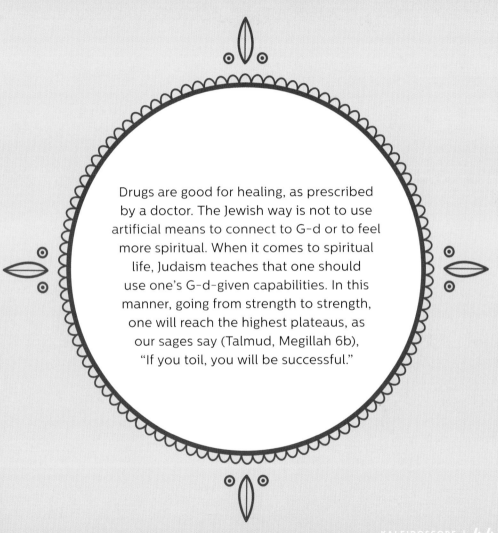

Drugs are good for healing, as prescribed by a doctor. The Jewish way is not to use artificial means to connect to G-d or to feel more spiritual. When it comes to spiritual life, Judaism teaches that one should use one's G-d-given capabilities. In this manner, going from strength to strength, one will reach the highest plateaus, as our sages say (Talmud, Megillah 6b), "If you toil, you will be successful."

EDUCATION

In 1978, President Jimmy Carter inaugurated Education Day U.S.A. in honor of the Rebbe's contributions to education. Celebrated on 11 Nissan, the Rebbe's Jewish birthday, it is still marked yearly with a presidential proclamation. In a letter to Vice President Walter F. Mondale, the Rebbe explained his philosophy of education:

Vice President Walter Mondale speaking at the event marking the first Education Day U.S.A. in 1978.

Education should not be limited to the acquisition of knowledge and preparation for a career; rather, its goal should be to teach a child how to live a better life, and to promote the betterment of society as a whole. Therefore, the educational system must pay more attention—indeed, this must be its central focus—to the building of character, with emphasis on moral and ethical values.

ELDERLY

The Rebbe rejected the idea of retirement for elderly people, arguing that it led them to be marginalized and to lose track of their purpose in life. He encouraged the establishment of learning circles for elderly men and women to study Jewish texts, and requested that the groups have a set schedule, designated place and curriculum. Bringing retirees together to study, rather than sit idle at home, would help underscore that they are a valuable part of the family unit:

Referring to someone as an "elder" should not be derogatory; on the contrary, the title indicates an advanced stage of understanding and knowledge. Younger generations ignore their elders at their own risk. Their wisdom can alleviate many doubts and much discord, and prevent many mistakes.

EXTROVERT

A survivor of Soviet oppression, Rabbi Hillel Pevzner arrived at the Chabad school in the Paris suburb of Brunoy in 1946, becoming a teacher there. Later he established a Jewish day school, where, among other duties, his job was to go door to door, recruiting students and raising funds. This level of activism did not come easily to him. "It is too much for my introverted personality!" he told the Rebbe, who responded (paraphrased): "By nature, I too am introverted; nevertheless, I knew it was essential, and reluctantly accepted upon myself to be active in public life." The Rebbe's immense sense of responsibility toward others was his defining characteristic. When a woman asked why Chabad men do not continue to study Torah full-time after marriage, as is the custom in many Chassidic circles, he replied that they are too busy helping other people:

Hillel the Elder famously said that the fundamental rule of the Torah is: "What is hateful to you, do not do to others." How would you feel if you were an assimilated Jew who wanted to learn about Judaism, but no one was available to help you, because they were all busy studying themselves? In these times, when intermarriage and assimilation are rampant, our primary responsibility is to keep Judaism alive. Even those who are not Chabad followers should ask themselves: Am I truly studying all day? Could my time be better spent helping those in need?

FEMININITY

The Rebbe encouraged women to accept leadership positions, especially in educational institutions. One of the first organizations he founded was the Lubavitch Women's Organization, which coordinates study groups, outreach events and programming:

One of the first Chabad women's conventions in the United States.

It is incumbent upon us to reach out to assimilated Jews and teach them about Judaism and their Jewish heritage. Women are blessed with an innate sympathetic and tender nature, which gives them an advantage in this endeavor.

FOOD

It's an established reality—and sometimes a humorous one—that much of Judaism is celebrated around a holiday table. Additionally, there are numerous laws regarding food. Many would say that there is nothing like fulfilling G-d's commandments via traditions that are connected with food. The Rebbe saw it not just as a physical pleasure in and of itself:

Before eating bread, we make a blessing to thank G-d for providing nourishment, and we have in mind the positive acts we'll complete with the energy we've gleaned. In Judaism, the spiritual is not disconnected from the material. This concept is expressed best in food, which, when eaten for holy purposes, integrates the spiritual into our physical bodies.

GATHERING

Among Chabad followers, the *farbrengen*, Chassidic gathering, is an essential component of divine service. The Rebbe encouraged that on every special occasion, people should gather together in small or large groups to share inspiring stories and words of Torah, and sing Chassidic melodies:

The *farbrengen* requires at least two people, as the verse states, "Will two walk together, unless they have agreed?" (Amos 3:3) In this way, one assists the other, strengthening and encouraging him or her to lead an exemplary life that earns the respect of others and sanctifies the name of G-d. The words shared should make people feel closer, not only to their fellows, but to G-d.

A farbrengen, *Chassidic gathering in Kfar Chabad, Israel, circa 1963.*

HARMONY

The first Chabad rebbe, Rabbi Schneur Zalman of Liadi, articulated a philosophy of trust in G-d, morality, and a deep responsibility to perfect the world. "Judaism places emphasis on action," the Rebbe wrote. "The purpose of knowledge is that it should lead to a mitzvah. Chabad philosophy goes a step further, explaining that every deed should be done, not just with the body, but with the soul, meaning with vitality and intention." He elaborated:

The soul descends to earth in order to reveal harmony in the world. The task begins with the person, who is called a "small world," integrating the spiritual and physical aspects of life. Chassidism teaches that by performing a holy act with the proper intention and feeling, one achieves the ultimate personal harmony: physical, spiritual, emotional and intellectual.

HOLIDAYS

Every moment of a Jewish holiday was precious to the
Rebbe. To be in his presence on a holiday was to enter a
realm of holiness, whether the tone of the day was joyous or
solemn. Mr. Benjamin Netanyahu, then Israel's ambassador
to the United Nations, described watching the Rebbe on
the holiday of Simchat Torah as an event he would "never
forget to the end of my life." The Rebbe's dance with the
Torah created a circle of light, he said. "I felt the strength of
generations, the power of our traditions, our faith and our
people." To the Rebbe, however, the significance of a holiday
was not just the day itself:

> > > > > > > > > > >

The Rebbe during the Sukkot holiday prayer services.

The intent and purpose of days that are out of the ordinary—the Jewish holidays—is that they should influence ordinary days. By telling their stories, studying their messages and reflecting on their themes, we spread the holidays throughout the year, and make them part of our daily lives.

HUMILITY

When people wrote to the Rebbe describing their accomplishments, expecting congratulations and praise, he would quote our sages: "One who has a hundred [dollars] wants two hundred; one who has two hundred wants four hundred." Achievement, he would say, whets the appetite for even greater achievement, and at a faster pace. If people claimed they did not have the capabilities to accomplish more, the Rebbe would respond that such an attitude was a misuse of humility. Humility does not mean deceiving yourself about your true abilities:

G-d gave you talents and capabilities. Recognize them and use them for good purposes. However, know that G-d gave them, and if He had chosen to bless someone else with them, perhaps—or surely—she or he would have used them better. Humility is the recognition that you are no greater than the next person, for your talents did not come from your own hands. This attitude will lead even the greatest individual to joyfully assist one who was not blessed in the same way. As G-d says (Isaiah 57:15), "With him that is of a contrite and humble spirit [I dwell]."

ILLUSTRATIONS

Written material for children should always be accompanied by illustrations, the Rebbe told artist Michel Schwartz. He emphasized that the art should be top-notch. In a 1982 letter he wrote that an artistic gift should be used not only to earn a living, but should also be "a vehicle to promote Judaism." The Rebbe took the time to review and comment on art that was published in Chabad magazines. To the children's magazine *Moshiach Times*, he described how he felt comics should be drawn:

A comic story by Joe Kubert for the Moshiach Times magazine.

It is hard to relate to a character drawn in an abnormal way—very fat, or with a long nose and limbs. When the purpose is to convey an educational message, the more normal, the simpler the character looks, the better the effect on a child, or even an adult.

Manuscripts of Chabad teachings.

INTELLECT

Many Chabad teachings remained unpublished until the middle of the 20th century. In 1977 the Rebbe decided to print *Ayin-Beit*, the monumental work of Rabbi Sholom DovBer, the fifth Chabad rebbe. This collection of discourses touches on every area of Jewish scholarship: creation, the world's constitution, purpose, the human psyche and faith. It shows Chabad philosophy to be a multifaceted approach to serving G-d:

To serve G-d with emotion or with faith is not enough. There must be a fusion of these elements, which can come only through intellect, for it rules over both. Do not be satisfied with an incomplete spiritual life. Serve G-d with your whole being.

JOY

Joy is critical to a healthy and balanced life. "Chassidism teaches and insists," the Rebbe told a group of students in 1960, "that everyone, man or woman, has an obligation to observe Judaism with joy and inspiration, not mechanically." The Rebbe stressed that joy and contentment flow from a realization that G-d created us for a purpose, that we have a mission in this world:

You would likely be joyous if the president of the United States were to appoint you to some important position. G-d placed His lofty spiritual worlds to the side, and said that they were all created for the sake of our world. Thus, you should be joyous, for the King of all kings has chosen you over another spiritual being to be His ambassador and to fulfill His requests.

JUSTICE

The Seven Noahide Laws are moral biblical directives from G-d to all mankind prior to the Jews' exodus from Egypt. They include obligations to acknowledge G-d's dominion and to establish courts of law. Historically, the laws were not publicized because Jews lived under oppressive regimes, and doing so would have put them in danger. In 1985 the Rebbe began a campaign to promote the Noahide Laws. He believed that though most civilized nations today recognize human rights and religious freedom, these basic tenets provide a missing link:

In our time, a nation that trumpeted human rights, and even animal rights, chose to perpetrate some of the cruelest acts humanity has ever seen. If the Germans would have recognized that G-d was watching them, a G-d who commanded them to not murder or steal, the Holocaust would not have been possible.

KINDNESS

Synagogues are commonly understood to be places of prayer, communal study and reflection. The Rebbe encouraged constant growth in these areas, but also suggested that synagogues become reservoirs of kindness, with the establishment of interest-free loan societies. A loan is a special form of charity, as it allows people to overcome a hardship without feeling ashamed at receiving a handout. The Rebbe also called on children to establish loan societies in their classrooms:

Every class should establish a free loan society. The children should donate to the fund and contribute their time to the society. The class should elect a president, treasurer and officers. Elections should happen often, and all the students should have the opportunity to be elected over the course of a school year. This will give the children a sense of responsibility towards the community, and will teach them to do kindness from a young age.

LANGUAGE

Mr. Frank Lautenberg, chairman of the United Jewish Appeal (UJA), visited the Rebbe in 1975 to discuss the organization's communal activities. After a long conversation, the Rebbe talked about *tefillin* (the black boxes worn on the arm and head during weekday prayers). Did Mr. Lautenberg wear them? He did not. In fact, he confessed, he could not read Hebrew, and would not be able to recite the blessings and prayers associated with the mitzvah. There was no need to wait on that account, the Rebbe told him. The prayers could be recited in English.

This philosophy of making Judaism accessible in as many languages as possible was a hallmark of the Rebbe's leadership. In 1956, Isaac Steinberg, a well-known Jewish author and politician, who had been a member of the Left Socialist Revolutionary Party during the Russian Revolution, phoned Chabad headquarters to complain. The Rebbe's letters were being translated into English and French, not just Hebrew and Yiddish, and Mr. Steinberg was not happy about it. "This will cause assimilation," the observant Jew told the Rebbe's aide. The Rebbe responded that he was pleased to hear that Mr. Steinberg was so bothered by assimilation, but he could not agree with him:

Language has nothing to do with assimilation. People could speak Hebrew and Yiddish and still be assimilated. To combat assimilation, we need to act quickly. We need to reach Jews in their languages and not wait until they learn Hebrew. Time lost in this critical work is time that cannot be returned.

TALKS AND TALES

MONTHLY

2nd Year ADAR I, 5703 Vol. II, No. 3

CONTENTS:

1. Events and Dates
2. Test Your Knowledge
3. Parshath Shekolim
4. The Mishkon
5. The Prophet Elijah
6. Tephillin
7. Rabbenu Tam
8. The "I" Opener
9. Things to Remember

Adar I
5703

Pr
5

A Chabad publication.

MERKOS L'INYONEI CHINUCH Inc.
770 EASTERN PARKWAY, BROOKLYN, N.Y.

LEADERSHIP

For a year after the passing of his father-in-law, the sixth Chabad rebbe, the Rebbe refused to accept the mantle of leadership, though he continued his involvement with the movement's educational branch. Many Chabad disciples beseeched him to accept the position, but he flatly refused. Only after his wife, Rebbetzin Chaya Mushka, implored him to consent lest her father's work be lost did he agree. The Rebbe constantly stressed that every individual needs to fulfill their mission on this world by him or herself. In his inaugural talk, in January 1951, he said:

A talk in the early 1950s, during the early years of the Rebbe's leadership.

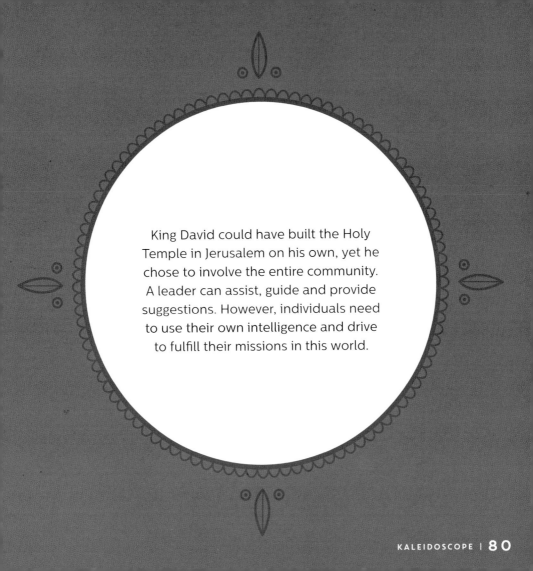

King David could have built the Holy Temple in Jerusalem on his own, yet he chose to involve the entire community. A leader can assist, guide and provide suggestions. However, individuals need to use their own intelligence and drive to fulfill their missions in this world.

The public Chanukah menorah on Fifth Avenue in New York City.

LIGHT

Despair was never a viable option to the Rebbe. He saw fully, perhaps more than others, the grave dangers of assimilation. But, rather than encouraging his followers to withdraw from the world and isolate themselves, he told them to reach out. In response to the darkness of secular American culture, he initiated a campaign to encourage more women, even young girls, to light Shabbat candles. In a Chanukah letter, the Rebbe explained why the menorah is kindled at night:

We kindle the Chanukah lights after sunset, when it is dark outside. When you find yourself "after sunset," when the light of day has given way to gloom and darkness—as it did for the Jews under oppressive Greek rule—do not despair, G-d forbid. Fortify yourself with complete trust in G-d, the essence of goodness; take heart in the firm belief that the darkness is only temporary and will soon be dispelled with a bright light.

LIVELIHOOD

Maimonides wrote that the greatest form of charity is to provide a needy person with a livelihood. The Rebbe constantly sought creative ways for people to earn an income, from commissioning an artist to produce work for a publication to connecting a jeweler with a group of Holocaust survivors to whom he taught jewelry-making. Yet, the Rebbe strongly affirmed, while one must be proactive in finding a livelihood, one's income, business or job should not become consuming:

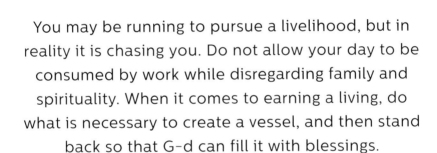

You may be running to pursue a livelihood, but in reality it is chasing you. Do not allow your day to be consumed by work while disregarding family and spirituality. When it comes to earning a living, do what is necessary to create a vessel, and then stand back so that G-d can fill it with blessings.

MAIMONIDES

In 1984 the Rebbe introduced a campaign to encourage the daily study of Maimonides' work on Jewish law, the *Mishneh Torah*. Its fourteen volumes contain a digest of *all* Jewish laws, including those that will be applicable during the messianic era. The Rebbe suggested several tracks of learning based on time availability, and even one for young children. In one talk, the Rebbe examined the introduction:

A vintage volume of Maimonides' work on Jewish law, the Mishneh Torah.

Maimonides chose to begin his magnum opus by quoting the verse: "In the name of the L-rd, the everlasting G-d" (Genesis 21:33). Although his volume is replete with brilliant scholarship, he expresses a firm belief that his talents were granted to him by G-d. He then adds the verse "Then shall I not be ashamed, when I have regard for all of Your commandments" (Psalms 119:6). How did Maimonides have the boldness to chronicle the entire corpus of Jewish law? He understood, as he explains in his introduction, that when G-d graces you with a talent, you cannot ignore it. Neglecting your talents is not modesty; rather, it is listening to your animalistic inclination to shy away from performing your mission in this world.

MATTER

Over the years the Rebbe corresponded with several scientists about matters of science and religion. He had studied science on the university level from 1928–1932 in Berlin, and from 1934–1938 in Paris. "I have tried to follow scientific developments in certain areas ever since," he wrote. There could be no contradiction between science and Judaism, the Rebbe reasoned, because science "is not in a position to offer ultimate truths" about large questions like the origin of the universe. Science sets its own limits, "declaring that its predictions are, and will always be, in every case, merely most probable, but not certain; it speaks only in terms of theories." The Rebbe drew on his knowledge of science to illuminate Torah concepts and statements of Jewish sages. In a 1986 talk, he discussed matter:

G-d created the world so that everything is made up of many atoms. At the center of each atom is the nucleus of protons and neutrons, surrounded by a cloud of orbiting electrons. Every creation, no matter how large or small, at the atomic level, is the same. This brings another dimension of meaning to the prayer we say during the High Holidays, that before G-d, the greatest celestial body, "large," and the granule of sand, "small," are equal.

This also opens a new perspective for us on the world. To our eyes, the world appears fractured, divided between good and evil, with evil prevailing more often than good. In truth, however, good and evil are unified under G-d, who is the one Source of everything.

MENTOR

Central to the teachings of Chassidism is the imperative to learn from everything one sees and hears, and from every person one meets. The Rebbe took this a step further, based on the teaching in *Ethics of Our Fathers* to "provide yourself with a teacher" (1:16). He encouraged every person to find a *mashpia*, a mentor to consult on important spiritual and material decisions:

When in doubt, we cannot rely on our own intellect to make the best objective decisions. Asking someone who has no personal bias will clear any doubt. Speaking to your mentor from time to time about where you stand spiritually will give you a perspective on which areas can be improved.

MERGERS

The Rebbe did not view mergers of synagogues and Jewish institutions in a positive light. When two synagogues in Manchester, England, wanted to reunite many years after a feud had caused the community to split, the Rebbe wrote to them, "This is the time when the number of synagogues should be increased rather than decreased." He expressed the same attitude in 1986, writing to the president of the National Council of Young Israel about a proposed merger of two national organizations in the name of Jewish unity. Although unity was a cause close to the Rebbe's heart, he did not favor the merger:

Every organization has its unique goals, its unique realm of activities and practical achievements. A merger could cause some of them to be neglected or forgotten. Every organization has its own standards. Mergers bring compromise, most of the time at the expense of Jewish ideals. Every organization is motivated not just by its own desire to do good, but by competition with others in the same field. When it comes to doing good, our sages say (Baba Batra 21a), "Jealousy between scholars increases wisdom." Every organization has the ability to critique other organizations. Why should all this be lost for the sake of unity?

MITZVAH

When Israel was on the verge of war in 1967, the Rebbe called on all Jews to increase their observance, specifically encouraging men to don *tefillin*, black boxes containing parchments inscribed with biblical verses. The Rebbe urged his followers to go out onto the streets to help Jews perform this mitzvah, and the campaign led thousands to put on *tefillin* for the first time. Every single Jew had to be reached, the Rebbe said. Even one positive act benefited the Jewish people as a whole:

>>>>>>>>>>

Donning tefillin on the streets of New York City during the Six-Day War.

The sages state that every person, even a wicked one, is filled with mitzvahs as a pomegranate is filled with seeds. This means that each deed creates an eternal bond with G-d that can never be severed, no matter what a person chooses to do afterward.

MORALITY

Children often feel that in the absence of a supervising adult, they can do as they please. The Rebbe felt that children need to be taught that there is a higher Being who is constantly watching. He wanted this to be included in the public-school curriculum, but laws regarding separation of church and state prevented it. Instead, the Rebbe encouraged a moment of silence:

At the start of the school day, students should observe a moment of silence. They should be guided to contemplate what is important to them. They will then question their parents, "What is most important? What should I be thinking about?" The parent will explain their beliefs, their faith in a Creator and the fact that He is constantly watching over us. This will create tangible changes in our children, our families and our society.

Children in public school observe a moment of silence.

MOSHIACH

If there was one issue that the Rebbe stressed, it was his desire to see the coming of the final redemption, the messianic era. When people asked how to bring that time of global peace and goodness, the Rebbe would respond simply: by doing more deeds of kindness. "What is the Messiah?" a *New York Times* reporter once asked him. The Rebbe responded:

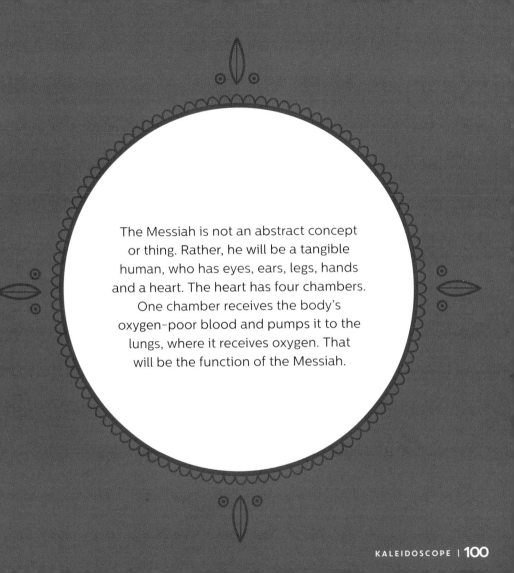

The Messiah is not an abstract concept or thing. Rather, he will be a tangible human, who has eyes, ears, legs, hands and a heart. The heart has four chambers. One chamber receives the body's oxygen-poor blood and pumps it to the lungs, where it receives oxygen. That will be the function of the Messiah.

NEIGHBORS

In the 1960s many Jewish neighborhoods across the United States began to deteriorate. Once-affluent areas became dangerous slums. As Jews fled, the communities continued to change. The flight affected real estate, businesses, synagogues, schools, charities and the elderly, many of whom did not have the resources to move. The Rebbe beseeched:

Think not of yourself, but of your neighbors. Ask, "What damage will I be causing them by leaving? What will happen to those who can't afford to move, or who don't have the strength to begin life anew?" Our sages said, "Do not do to others what you don't want done to you."

OBSTACLES

As Chabad-Lubavitch continued to grow, there became a clear need for a volunteer branch that would organize ongoing activities. Thus the Lubavitch Youth Organization in North America was born. The Rebbe addressed difficulties that might hinder the organization's progress:

Many times, meetings beget more meetings, which beget more meetings. To achieve results, there must be action immediately after the first meeting. Do not fear the possibility of failure, as it is a lesson for the future. The fourth Chabad rebbe, Rabbi Shmuel, said, "The world says that if there is no way to go under, go over. I say that one should leap over from the start." Instead of allowing challenges to discourage you, disregard them and move forward joyously, without looking back.

OUTREACH

The Rebbe created and led a movement to reach every Jew in the world. He spent many of his talks emphasizing the danger that assimilation posed to Jewish survival and encouraging his followers to fight it with all their strength. Unlike others involved in Jewish outreach, he did not see his work as reaching out to "those who are far" from the right way of life. Nor did he see it as "bringing back those who have strayed." For who, the Rebbe asked, can determine who is far and who is near? A lack of Jewish education does not make one any less a Jew, he emphasized: "All Jews have a 'Jewish background.' They are descendants of Abraham, Isaac and Jacob, of Sarah, Rebecca, Rachel and Leah." In 1989, the Rebbe told a businessman:

>>>>>>>>>>>

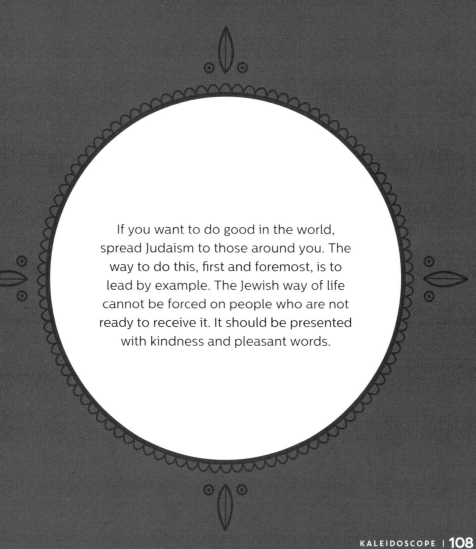

If you want to do good in the world, spread Judaism to those around you. The way to do this, first and foremost, is to lead by example. The Jewish way of life cannot be forced on people who are not ready to receive it. It should be presented with kindness and pleasant words.

PARENTS

Rabbi Levi Yitzchak Schneerson, the Rebbe's father, was exiled to a remote location in the Soviet Union as punishment for his efforts on behalf of the Jewish community. He passed away in 1944. The Rebbe's mother, Rebbetzin Chana, arrived in the United States in 1947. The Rebbe's respect for his parents was boundless. He visited his mother daily, and was careful to never turn his back to her. In 1964, in commemoration of the 20th anniversary of his father's passing, he began an initiative to establish an interest-free loan society for Jewish schools and parents. Regarding the commandment to honor one's parents, he explained:

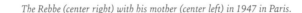

The Rebbe (center right) with his mother (center left) in 1947 in Paris.

It is a logical principle to respect those who gave us life and sustenance from an early age. However, there is another dimension to honoring our parents, and it is that G-d is also a partner in our creation. G-d commands us to honor our parents, and by fulfilling the commandment, we honor G-d too.

PEACE

The Rebbe saw conflict, between people or nations, as a sign that mankind had forgotten its Creator. G-d created the world "with kindness, love and mercy," he pointed out, and called for people to emulate these qualities. G-d endowed the world with ample resources, he said in a 1990 talk. Recognizing that the resources are a divine gift, and preserving and dividing them accordingly, would "remove the basis for strife and division among nations." Acknowledging G-d's presence creates internal peace as well, the Rebbe explained:

The question of why G-d created the world must be answered on two levels: one logical, the other illogical. The logical answer is that He created the world so that we should perfect it using the tools He gave us—our physical bodies, intellectual capabilities and emotional attributes. The second, illogical answer is that G-d wanted to have a "dwelling place," a home, in the physical world. These two answers imply two corresponding forms of divine service. In one, we study Torah and perform mitzvahs in order to make the world a better, holier place. In the other, we do these things for no other reason than that G-d commanded us to. Ultimately, we strive to blend both kinds of service.

PEER PRESSURE

In America, Jews found freedom of religion, but also a pervasive secular culture that was almost impossible to resist. The Rebbe encouraged Jews to renew their Jewish identity, in both private and public life. Acknowledging that the pressure to conform was intense, he explained that Jews should learn positive traits from their neighbors, and discard negative ones. To a group of Jewish children who wanted to go to public school like their neighborhood friends, he said:

What did Noah do when building the ark? Did he succumb to peer pressure? What did our forefather Abraham do? Did he try to fit in to the idolatrous atmosphere in which he was raised? What did Moses do? Was he influenced by his Egyptian surroundings? We can learn from our great Jewish leaders to ignore peer pressure and do what we know is right.

The Rebbe during prayer services.

PRAYER

Chabad teachings emphasize the importance of praying with concentration and intention. The Rebbe suggested that people should choose one part of the daily service and make an effort to concentrate on the meaning of the words. People who cannot understand the Hebrew should have in mind that they are praying to G-d. He also urged people to look at the words in the prayerbook rather than reciting them from memory. The Rebbe himself prayed with his eyes glued to the page, many times pointing to the words with his finger. Addressing the larger subject, he once asked: Why do we need to pray? If we deserve what we are asking for, should G-d not give it without our asking? And if we are not deserving, why even ask? The answer, he explained, depends on how we pray:

By praying, we acknowledge that everything we need and desire comes from G-d. The prayer service brings us to contemplate G-d's greatness and kindness, and when we do, we ourselves are elevated, becoming better, kinder people, worthy of receiving our requests.

PREVENTION

The Rebbe encouraged taking preemptive action in all areas of life. In education, and in spiritual endeavors, he urged people to anticipate negative situations that might arise, and step in to prevent them. "Curing the sick is surely an impressive and difficult feat," the Rebbe wrote. With preemptive care, "no one gets to celebrate the patient's recovery and the wonder of medicine. However, we will all surely agree that preventing something is much better." In 1968, the Rebbe explained to Mayor John Lindsay that preempting crime is very important:

Providing proper protection and security is not only good for potential victims of crime. It is, in fact, more beneficial for the perpetrators. When they are prevented from committing crimes, they avoid all the repercussions, such as criminal records, jail time, etc., and gain the opportunity to become good citizens.

PRIDE

After the Holocaust, many Jews limited their observance to the home and synagogue. The Rebbe, however, stated that keeping Judaism private would do nothing to combat anti-Semitism and assimilation. One of his first initiatives was a parade celebrating Jewish pride and unity. Until today, children from Jewish day schools and public schools march down Eastern Parkway in Brooklyn with banners promoting Jewish themes and observances. The Nazis proved that even European Jews who concealed their Jewish identity were found out, the Rebbe wrote. There is no benefit in hiding one's Judaism; on the contrary, being proud will compel others to respect you for your religious convictions:

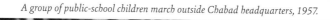

A group of public-school children march outside Chabad headquarters, 1957.

Practicing Judaism openly evokes pride and a spirit of Jewish identity in the unaffiliated. There is no reason to hide one's Jewishness in this free country. Public practice of Judaism is in keeping with the American slogan *e pluribus unum*, "out of many, one." The American culture has been enriched by the thriving ethnic cultures that contribute, each in its own way, to American life, both materially and spiritually.

A clandestine prayer service in the Soviet Union.

PRIORITIES

The Chabad movement wasn't welcome in the Soviet Union. Many Chabad activists, including the sixth Chabad rebbe, Rabbi Yosef Yitzchak Schneersohn, were jailed and expelled from the country. As Jews worldwide protested the fate of Russian Jewry, Chabad's clandestine network continued to operate. The Rebbe maintained secret communication with his followers in the country, and sent emissaries posing as tourists to teach Torah and deliver ritual items. Living in constant danger, one 17-year-old wrote to the Rebbe. He did not ask about his material needs, which were surely not being met, or his fears regarding the future; instead, he wrote that he had difficulty concentrating during prayer, and asked for advice. The Rebbe repeated the story to his followers, along with this message:

Let's learn about our priorities. We live in a free and democratic country. We have an abundance of material good, and we practice our religion freely. Yet we complain that we do not have enough livelihood. There are Jews who live behind the Iron Curtain in poverty, yet they are not concerned with material needs. Every Jewish observance is an act of great self-sacrifice. They save potatoes for Passover so they will have what to eat. They worry all week about how they will miss school and work on Shabbat and Jewish holidays without getting into trouble with the authorities. This is the comparison we need to make when calculating our material assets.

Conversation with a Jewish inmate.

PRISON

It can be easy to forget those behind bars. Sometimes their actions are abhorrent and have brought harm to many people. But the Rebbe felt strongly that this segment of society should not be neglected, and encouraged outreach toward Jewish inmates. Years later, he explained his reasoning to Israeli Prime Minister Yitzhak Rabin:

The purpose of prison should not be to simply punish the inmates. The experience should bring the prisoner to regret the past and establish a future that is free of crime and wrongdoing. Even when still imprisoned, he or she should become, mentally and spiritually, a free person, so that when the term is over, returning to a normal life will not be difficult.

PROTECTION

Whenever he could, the Rebbe would encourage people to increase their Jewish observance, often urging them to go "from strength to strength," (Psalms 84:8). He once wrote to a London businessman that "the laws of the Torah were given not for the benefit of the Creator, but for the benefit of the observer, for good health, both physically and spiritually." In 1974, the Rebbe explained this concept using an analogy from the life of a soldier:

Soldiers wear helmets. The helmets are heavy and cumbersome, and training is required to use them properly. But the soldiers wear them anyway, for one day the helmets may save their lives. Mitzvahs are like a helmet. At times, they may seem a heavy, useless burden, but do not give up. Persevere in your observance, for there will come a day when their true worth will be revealed.

PURPOSE

In talks, discourses and correspondence, the Rebbe stressed that our purpose is to make a "home for G-d" in this physical world. This fundamental concept in Chabad philosophy comes from the statement by our sages, "G-d desired to have a dwelling place here below." The Rebbe explained:

There are two dimensions at looking at why G-d created the world. One that there was a reason, such as to make us better people. There is another dimension of service that is above our understanding, which is G-d's unexplainable desire for a fitting "dwelling place." This, too, G-d wants us to accomplish by serving Him in a way that is beyond our comprehension. However, in this material world, G-d wants us to use our skills—our intellect and emotions—to fulfill His will, as in the first dimension. Ultimately, we strive toward blending both kinds of service, that we fulfill G-d's will because He desired, but that G-d also wants us to understand and fulfill His will in our physical being and understanding.

RACISM

In the 1960s, West Indians and African Americans began moving into Crown Heights, Brooklyn, which had been predominantly Jewish for decades. Many Jews immediately fled the neighborhood. When someone asked if he should move, the Rebbe responded that in every group of people there are those who choose to act immorally. "There is nothing to panic from. They are the same as us, and you could live with them peacefully." In the fall of 1989, the Rebbe explained to then New York mayoral candidate David Dinkins that Judaism does not tolerate racism:

G-d created all people for the purpose of doing good, beginning with themselves and their families. Defining people by race is unnecessary and meaningless. America is called a "melting pot." The pot should bubble so actively that differences in skin color or country of origin become insignificant.

Mayor David Dinkins (left) meets with the Rebbe, 1990.

REBUILDING

Though the Rebbe and his wife, Rebbetzin Chaya Mushka, narrowly escaped the Holocaust, they lost close relatives. In the United States, the sixth Chabad rebbe, Rabbi Yosef Yitzchak Schneersohn, worked tirelessly to save European Jews and to rebuild Judaism after the war. Upon Rabbi Yosef Yitzchak's passing in 1950, the Rebbe continued his legacy. He wrote to Holocaust survivor and Nobel laureate Elie Wiesel:

It is no doubt an obligation to never forget what our enemies have done to us, but it is no less an obligation to fight the assimilation that is plaguing the Jewish nation. We need to be active in rebuilding our people by bringing Jewish children into the world, promoting Jewish education and teaching by example.

REBUKE

"A person is a mirror" is one of the classic teachings of the founder of Chassidism, Rabbi Israel ben Eliezer, known as the Baal Shem Tov. He taught that when you notice a negative trait in another, you are actually seeing your own flaws reflected in that person. But, the Rebbe asked, isn't there a biblical command to rebuke your fellow? Isn't our mission in this world not just to help ourselves, but others too?

When you see someone do something wrong, there are two ways to look at it. The first is to cast aspersions on the character of the person: he has negative traits that need to be rectified; she has flaws that need to be fixed. The other is to see the action as separate from the person: here is a good person who needs help to get back on the right track.

One who takes the first approach is indeed looking into a mirror. One who takes the second may safely offer a gentle rebuke, for it will be a rebuke born of love.

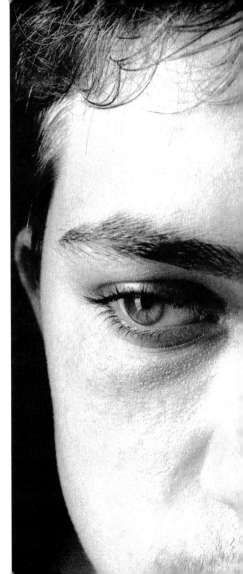

REDEMPTION

For thousands of years Jews have yearned for the time when suffering will end and G-d's presence will be openly revealed. The Rebbe recognized that the world was moving toward a better time, when peace would reign, and poverty, starvation and illness would become distant memories. Though it seemed an unattainable dream, he insisted that the combined effort of many individuals could make it real. Every deed of kindness brings redemption closer, the Rebbe explained:

>>>>>>>>>>>

The world was created for you, so that you can perform your G-d-given mission. Just as each person has a specific mission, so too each moment has a purpose. You may think, "What am I doing here now? Could I not be doing better elsewhere?" Focus on where you are now. Strive to bring completion and holiness into your immediate surroundings.

REPENTANCE

The Rebbe pointed out that the Hebrew word *teshuvah* does not mean "repentance," though it is often translated that way. Regret and remorse are part of the process of *teshuvah*, he explained, but they are only the first step. The true translation of the word is "return." Every person is inherently good. People may lose touch with the goodness and holiness within them, but it is always possible to return to their true selves and to their Creator. The Rebbe emphasized many times that *teshuvah* should never lead to despondency. Once, when the Rebbe asked someone why he looked glum, the man replied that he was upset because he had sinned. Immediately, the Rebbe responded:

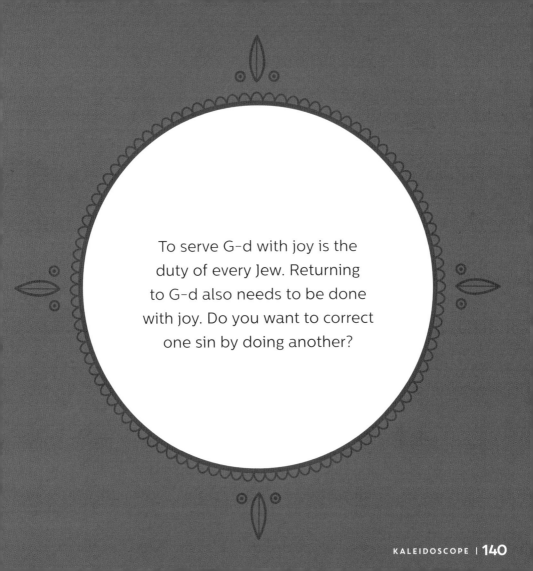

To serve G-d with joy is the
duty of every Jew. Returning
to G-d also needs to be done
with joy. Do you want to correct
one sin by doing another?

RESPECT

Thousands of letters poured into the Rebbe's office every week. It was a difficult task to review and answer them all. Many contained private information or requests, and the Rebbe wanted to open them himself. If he asked his aides to respond for him, he would cut out any sensitive information from the letters, leaving only the name. Once an aide suggested that perhaps the many congratulatory letters the Rebbe sent for births, marriages and bar and bat mitzvahs should be signed with a rubber stamp, which would save much time. The Rebbe rejected the idea:

When an individual takes the time to write a letter to inform me of a happy occasion, how would he or she feel to receive good wishes that were not personally signed, but rather mechanically stamped?

The Rebbe at a public gathering, with a pen in hand.

RESPONSIBILITY

In 1965 the young Yehoshua Mondshine wrote to Chabad headquarters about the need for a new Jewish youth magazine in Israel. "The major youth magazines [are] shuttered," he wrote. "This vacuum needs to be filled, and it should be done by Chabad." The Rebbe's response came a few months later. "If you have the possibility to fill that void with a newspaper...you should take care to see that all the logistics are possible, that there is funding, and once all is in place, come back with a proposal and it will be evaluated." The point was well taken. If you have an idea, step up to the plate. On the same note, the Rebbe wrote to someone in 1966:

The plans are good. If only, at the end, there will be those who will cooperate with you. It is understood, however, that the others' lack of action, at least for now, places a greater responsibility —and merit—on your shoulders. If no one is helping you, intensify your involvement.

RETIREMENT

Prior to his 70th birthday, the Rebbe received a barrage of letters advising him to reduce his responsibilities and consider retirement. Instead, he asked his followers for a birthday present: 71 new Chabad institutions to be opened that year. "Age makes my life more exacting," he told the New York Times. "My age is demanding more of me." The Rebbe explained this in a talk on his birthday:

>>>>>>>>>>

The Rebbe presides over the gathering in honor of his 70th birthday.

"You are in this world to care and toil," G-d told Adam. G-d created the world in a way that requires us to work for our physical and spiritual needs. The Torah considers it shameful to receive a reward without working for it, since we become partners with G-d when we labor. To the best of their abilities, people should continue to work as they grow older.

SELF-MOTIVATION

The Rebbe spent countless hours speaking and corresponding with people. His lengthy scholarly talks would often end with new campaigns, which he urged his followers to carry out. Yet he would oft repeat, "I do not give commands." When Chabad in Israel drafted a letter to supporters who had volunteered to deliver lectures, it began "You are asked to be at...," with a location, date and time for the lecture. The Rebbe corrected the draft, writing, "We suggest that you be at..." In 1954, the administration of the Rabbinical College of Canada asked the Rebbe to send students from New York to boost their enrollment. He responded that he could not force students to go there. People need to act on their own volition, he wrote:

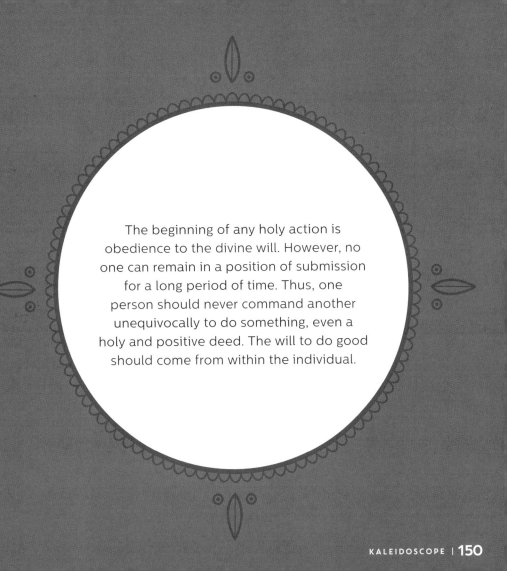

The beginning of any holy action is obedience to the divine will. However, no one can remain in a position of submission for a long period of time. Thus, one person should never command another unequivocally to do something, even a holy and positive deed. The will to do good should come from within the individual.

SIGHT

What we see affects us. Looking at holy things will have a positive effect, while looking at things which are not good will have a negative one. This is especially true with children, the Rebbe said:

Non-kosher animals exhibit negative traits—many are predators or scavengers—and one should refrain from looking at them unnecessarily. This is especially important for young children, as the verse states, "Educate the child according to his way, so that when he is old he will not depart from it" (Proverbs 22:6). From birth, and even before, a child should be surrounded by kosher imagery. Of course a child may see pictures of non-kosher animals to learn what not to eat, or visit the zoo to learn about the world and appreciate G-d's great creation. However, as much as possible, it is best to avoid bringing dolls and pictures of non-kosher animals into the home.

Entertainment for children at a parade in front of Chabad headquarters, 1987.

SPEECH

The Rebbe often pointed out that the Torah avoids negative language, choosing to negate a positive term ("not good"), rather than use a negative one ("bad"). Taking the same approach, the Rebbe encouraged the director of the Sheba Medical Center, Israel's largest hospital, not to call the institution a "house of the sick" (the Hebrew term for a hospital), but rather a "house of healing." Although it was a simple change of words, the Rebbe wrote, it "could affect how people see the center, as a place of healing, not sickness." In a 1966 talk, the Rebbe explained why avoiding negative speech is important:

Speaking brings our thoughts into the open and gives them a life of their own. Speaking negatively about another for the sake of idle talk injures the person who speaks, the listener and the person who is spoken about. Speaking positively about another, however, brings out the best in that person, effectively creating more goodness and kindness in the world.

SONG

Chabad teachings place great emphasis on music, and the Chabad repertoire of *nigunim*, melodies intended to uplift and inspire, is extensive. The Rebbe himself taught 13 *nigunim*, most of them Chabad songs that had been forgotten or that he had heard from Chassidic luminaries. In 1961 he taught *An'im Zemiros*, a powerful, soul-stirring melody with the Hebrew words "I sing hymns and compose songs because my soul longs for You. My soul desires Your shelter, to know all Your ways." The Rebbe related that he had learned it years earlier, when he observed a man sitting in the synagogue late into the night, so engrossed in the *nigun* that he did not notice that the fast of Yom Kippur had ended. On the power of song, the Rebbe said:

A choir sings Chassidic melodies at a 1977 concert in London.

Melody is the quill of the soul. Words may be an expression of your heart, but a melody expresses the contents of your soul. A good melody not only expresses the soul but, like a quill in hand, it brings one to action.

TEACHING

When the Rebbe's mother, Rebbetzin Chana, passed away, he chose to honor her memory by delivering scholarly talks on the biblical commentator Rabbi Shlomo Yitzchaki, known as Rashi. The Rebbe's talks fill over 200 volumes, and a large percentage of them are in-depth analyses of the commentary, which the Rebbe elucidated based on specific rules and guidelines. According to Rashi, his commentary is intended to be accessible to a child, yet it contains multiple dimensions that scholars have been exploring since its original publication:

Rabbi Shlomo Yitzchaki was a great scholar and authority on Jewish law. He was also a famed teacher who educated some of the greatest Talmudic scholars of his generation. Rashi's prized commentary, however, was intended to be understandable to a five-year-old student. This is the sign of a great leader: despite his tremendous scholarship, he cared for the smallest child.

TECHNOLOGY

The technological revolution of the 20th century presented both challenges and opportunities for observant Jews. While many shunned technology as a negative influence and a distraction from Jewish life, the Rebbe embraced it. Chabad has used every form of modern communication, from telephone hookups to livestreaming, to disseminate Torah and information about Jewish observance:

A Chabad rabbi conducts an interview live on the radio.

Everything that G-d created is potentially good. Certainly, technology that allows a person to be heard at the other end of the world has the potential to be utilized for good. It is our free choice to use technology for its intended purpose—to spread goodness and holiness—or, G-d forbid, the opposite.

TERROR

In 1956 terrorists entered Kfar Chabad, a small village near Tel Aviv inhabited by many survivors of Soviet Russia and Nazi Germany. Shooting indiscriminately, the terrorists murdered five students and a teacher at the village's vocational school. In response, the Rebbe sent a group of students to comfort the community with a message:

There is no explanation, theological or otherwise, for what happened. The question "Why?" must be answered with silence. However, you can be comforted by continuing to build the village and its institutions. This is the appropriate response to tragedy. To despair is to capitulate to the terrorists.

The rebuilt Chabad vocational school in Kfar Chabad, Israel.

UNITY

In 1982, a year after he launched a campaign for every Jewish child to have a letter in a Torah scroll, the Rebbe expanded the initiative to adults. That year many new Torah scrolls were written across the globe. The Rebbe explained why the project was unique:

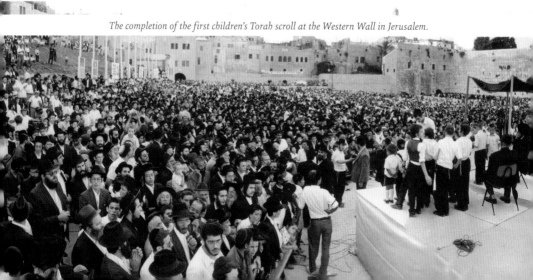

The completion of the first children's Torah scroll at the Western Wall in Jerusalem.

We must love our neighbors as we do ourselves, while appreciating and preserving our diversity. Every community has unique traditions, and every person is an individual, yet we are one people with one Torah. When thousands of people contribute financially to the writing of a Torah, their distinct identities combine to express G-d's will and wisdom. It exemplifies what our sages say: G-d, the Torah and the Jewish nation are all one.

UPLIFT

To promote Jewish pride, the Rebbe encouraged and attended grand parades in front of Chabad headquarters. The organization of the parades took much work, and was headed by Rabbi Yaakov Yehudah Hecht of the National Committee for the Furtherance of Jewish Education. Before the 1987 parade, Rabbi Hecht was worried. There were technical difficulties with the execution, and turnout was expected to be low.

Everything went smoothly, however, afterward he commented to the Rebbe that the unexpectedly large turnout had "schlepped him out" of his unfounded worries. No, the Rebbe corrected, the turnout had "lifted him" above his worries. The Rebbe explained that for the same reason, when Noah faced the great challenges of his generation, G-d uplifted him by praising his righteousness:

Praise encourages and uplifts the one who hears it.
A kind word can reveal hidden strengths.

The Rebbe expresses his satisfaction with the parade, 1987.

WEALTH

Many consider wealth a hindrance to divine service. Being rich makes one soft, dependent on physical comforts and less sensitive to spirituality. The Rebbe, however, argued that the challenges of wealth were preferable to those of poverty, and could, with G-d's help, be overcome. "A Jew needs to make every effort to be rich in spiritual pursuits and in material wealth in order to be able to perform all of the mitzvahs with peace of mind, and to be able to give a lot of charity," he said in 1992. The Rebbe stressed that being rich is a merit and a responsibility:

>>>>>>>>>>>

The Rebbe delivers a talk to Chabad donors.

G-d grants wealthy people the unique potential to contribute to the world, to help those around them. Just as when a person does his or her job successfully the employer will assign more duties, so too, when one uses wealth for G-dly purposes, G-d rewards and entrusts one with more wealth to use.

WOMEN

To those who questioned whether Judaism treats women equitably, the Rebbe responded that women's unique role in Jewish life makes them in some ways more important than men. Jewish life centers on the home, not the synagogue. The home is where the majority of observance takes place, and where the lives of children are shaped. Women are the ones who create the home and set the tone for the household. For this reason they were given the commandment of lighting candles:

> > > > > > > > > > >

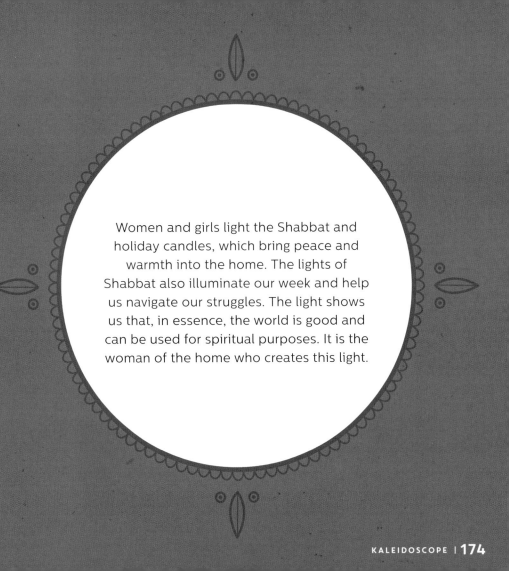

Women and girls light the Shabbat and holiday candles, which bring peace and warmth into the home. The lights of Shabbat also illuminate our week and help us navigate our struggles. The light shows us that, in essence, the world is good and can be used for spiritual purposes. It is the woman of the home who creates this light.

THE REBBE AND HIS COURT

By Harvey Swados

Before I learned in the winter of 1964 that the Lubavitcher Rebbe, Rabbi Menachem Mendel Schneerson, the then sixty-two-year-old leader of Hasidic Jewry, would receive me in audience, I had made several visits to these devout Jews' Brooklyn Headquarters. The modest brick building, between Flatbush and Crown Heights on Eastern Parkway, houses publishing offices, a school for children, a *yeshivah* for young men and a substantial auditorium.

My first visit was merely to introduce myself to their public relations man, a pleasant, bearded young Boston Latin School graduate named Yehuda Krinsky. It was at his suggestion that I paid my second visit, some weeks later, on the occasion of a *farbrengen*, a traditional gathering of the adherents of this two-hundred-year-old movement to discuss developments, recount tales of rabbis, and bolster each other in the faith.

The one that I attended is an annual event, commemorating the miraculous release of the late Rebbe from a Soviet prison. It is often swelled by the arrival of chartered planeloads of Hasidic Jews from abroad.

THE HASIDIC GATHERING

When I arrived, at about eight-thirty, and made my way past the Irish cops chatting amiably with clusters of orthodox Jews whose earlocks hung down beneath their broad-brimmed hats, the crowd of faithful and curious was already dense, and the Rebbe had just made his way to the dais.

The Rebbe in his office, 1965.

The view from the Rebbe's dais, 1968.

The ceremonial of oratory, toasts, and singing would go on uninterruptedly for five or six hours.

I had been prepared for a crowd, but not for this crushing mob of bearded males, many of them like myself in winter overcoats which they could not possibly raise their arms to remove; nor for the little seven- and eight-year-olds, their heads uniformly covered with skullcaps, squeezed and swaying so that I feared for their safety.

Someone recognized me as an invited guest, and I was passed along through a side entrance, and so found myself wedged on a corner of the platform not six feet from the Rebbe, who was addressing the throng from a chair in which he was seated behind a long table covered with a white cloth, and flanked by two rows of the dignified, black-frocked elders of the Hasidic movement.

Looking out at the congregants, I saw what the Rebbe must have seen: a most remarkable assemblage, and one which for my part I shall never forget.

Seated facing at each other at three long tables, also covered with linen cloths on which stood an occasional bottle of Tokay Kosher wine, a dish of cookies, a paper sack filled with cakes, were several hundred men, ranging in age from their twenties to their seventies. Some were in business suits, others in the elegant black dressing gown that a pious Hasid wears for festive occasions, tied in the middle with a *gartel*, the sash that symbolizes the separation of man's higher mental and spiritual qualities from the inferior ones.

Perhaps nine out of ten were bearded—not for convenience, or perhaps vanity, as I was myself, but in accordance with religious prescriptions—and for some moments I was lost in contemplation of the immense variety of thickets, red, brown, black, gray, some sparse, others extravagantly luxuriant, in which many of their wearers allowed their fingers to stray, thoughtfully and proudly.

But as I freed myself from contemplation of the panorama of beards over the white tables, I became aware of the younger men closely packed against either wall, standing on raised planks like bleachers, of the many hundreds wedged tightly together at the rear of the hall, among whom I too had been squashed, and of those in the balcony, which was concealed from the rest of us by tinted glass— because, I realized, it was reserved for female congregants, some carrying little ones, their noses pressed to the glass. I became aware, too, of how these hundreds thronged together were attending, with a kind of passionate patience, to the speech of the Rebbe, who was addressing them calmly and steadily in a fluent Yiddish, without rising or raising his voice.

Since I could not follow the complex line of his discourse, with its parables taken from traditional Hasidic tales and homely incidents, interwoven with abstruse philosophical theory, I was free to stare at all those around me—rabbis, merchants,

Dignitaries join a gathering with the Rebbe, circa 1975.

scholars, small businessmen, students, workmen—who were listening with an intensity I had never encountered, whether in a classroom, at the public lectern, or at a religious or political rally.

Several teenage boys, their beards just starting to sprout, their eyes half-closed, trancelike, unseeing, swayed back and forth rapidly from the waist up, almost as if their torsos were propelled by some independent internal motor, in the contained ecstasy of their participation in the Rebbe's peroration.

Behind me, his hands clasped in his lap as he listened, quite motionless, sat Professor Paul Rosenblum, a well-known mathematician from the University of Minnesota. Just below me, Rabbi Mendel Futerfas, a sturdy rough-hewn man hunched over the table in profound thought as if carved of wood, his shaggy brows and greying beard shaded by the peak of a Russian workman's cap of the kind that one sees in old photographs of Russian revolutionaries and litterateurs. Who could he be? I discovered later that he had been released only two weeks before from twenty years of captivity in Soviet prison camps (where he had gained extraordinary renown for selfless generosity), and that he had flown from London relatives directly to this *farbrengen* in order that he might listen to the Rebbe.

Meanwhile the Rebbe, having concluded his first address of the evening, moistened his lips with the wine glass, and accepted, with a smiling inclination of the head, toasts eagerly offered him by those about him. It was then that the singing began.

At first spontaneous, soon encouraged and "conducted" by the Rebbe, who swung his forearms gaily, rhythmically to the beat of the music from his seated position, the simple song rose to a pitch of unrestrained enthusiasm, with the chorus repeated ten, fifteen times, each time wilder and faster. A man would have had to be made of stone not to respond to this great release of joyous energy. I did not know the words, but I found myself singing along with all those who showed their teeth through their beards bobbing from side to side in time to

The Rebbe (right) leads the singing at a gathering, 1968.

The crowd listens intently to the Rebbe's talk, 1968.

the music, often hopping up and down as well.

Suddenly, at the slightest of signals from the Rebbe, everyone fell silent. Refreshed and restored, they reverted to their posture of rapt attentiveness while the Rebbe resumed speaking for another three quarters of an hour. Fascinated by this alternation of intense intellectual virtuosity and physical release through song (the Rebbe continued speaking, I was told later, until about three o'clock in the morning), I stayed until perhaps midnight before going off to a neighborhood Hasidic hangout with a warm-hearted young Lubavitcher.

THE PRIVATE AUDIENCE

I had seen two aspects of Rabbi Schneerson, the coolly analytical and the gaily earthy; in each role he was the charismatic leader, gaining the rapt devotion of his followers. Others had told me that this scholar-philosopher, fluent in some ten languages and an engineering graduate, who studied at the Sorbonne before he accepted the task of leadership of the Lubavitcher Hasidim, was even more impressive—if more difficult to see—in private conversation.

I jumped at the opportunity to talk with the Rebbe, even though my appointment was for eleven o'clock on the night of what turned out to be the winter's fiercest snowstorm. Not only was my wife given welcome shelter in the building from the blinding snow—there were no other women in sight, at this late hour the last of the *yeshivah* students were still droning away in sing-song at their studies—but the Rebbe himself greeted her most kindly.

"We don't discriminate here," he said with a smile, and after he bade us seat ourselves before his desk, he inquired, in an English that was heavily accented but more fluent than my own, whether I would mind if he answered my questions in Yiddish.

Rabbi Schneerson's office was as bleak as the rest of the dingy building, the bare Venetian blinds drawn against the beating snow outside, the walls bare also, and with nothing on his desk but a pad and a telephone.

The Rebbe sat very still, attending to my queries with his head bent forward so that his broad-brimmed hat shaded his face, which appeared deceptively ruddy. He is a strikingly handsome man, whose almost classically regular features are not at all obscured by a graying beard which is full but not bushy, and whose pale blue eyes remain fixed upon you with an unblinking directness that can be disconcerting.

He rather reminds one of a Rembrandt rabbi in the shadowed planes of his composed countenance, which is not simply dignified but somber in repose; and yet the tilt of his hat seems at times almost rakish, and the glint of his eyes under its brim puts you in mind of those gifted bohemians of 19th-century Paris whom one encounters in Impressionist portraits. It is easy to imagine the figure he must have cut as a young man at the Sorbonne.

THE HOLOCAUST AND ISRAEL

I began by asking his opinion of the causes of the Holocaust which resulted in the extinction of six million European Jews—and of the controversy about the behavior of the German masses and the Jewish leadership, which has tormented the Western world ever since, particularly since the appearance of Hannah Arendt's book on the Eichmann trial. His reply made no reference to abstractions, whether theological or philosophical, nor did he remark on the sins the victims must have committed to be punished so terribly by G-d. He pointed instead to political realities, to the incredible difficulties in maintaining one's faith under a totalitarian regime.

Speaking of the hardship and the anguish

The Rebbe with New York City Council member Paul R. Screvane, 1965.

A private audience, 1965.

undergone by the Jews of communist Russia, he asked rhetorically: How much more difficult do you suppose it was to keep hold of one's integrity under the crushing weight of the German tyrants, who were so much more efficient than the Russians? No, he said firmly, the miracle was that there was any resistance at all, that there was any organization at all, that there was any leadership at all.

This was not exactly what I had expected. Was it his opinion, then, that the tragedy was not a unique visitation upon the Jewish people, and that it could happen again?

"Tomorrow morning," he replied unhesitatingly.

Why was he so certain? The Rebbe launched into an analysis of the German atrocities in a rhetoric that shifted eloquently and unhesitatingly, often in the same sentence, from English (for my benefit) to Yiddish (for nuance and precision). He did not speak mystically, nor did he harp on the German national character and its supposed affinity for Jew-hatred. Rather, he insisted upon the Germans' obedience to authority and their unquestioning carrying out of orders— even the most bestial—as a cultural-historical phenomenon that was the product of many generations of deliberate inculcation.

Then what future did he envision for the Jewish people? Would it not seem that they would tend to polarize—either to return to Israel, the land of their fathers, or to amalgamate with the general populace of such countries as the United States and Russia?

The Rebbe smiled. "No," he replied, "in my experience, the Jewish people have been moving from left to right."

Coming from his lips, the expression had almost a political ring to it. At my evident puzzlement, he repeated the phrase, which I took to mean that he had been witnessing a kind of religious revival among the new generation of Jewry.

In this connection, I was most curious to learn what this distinguished leader of Hasidic Jewry, consulted not only by humble followers desiring his blessing and his counsel on personal problems, but also by such political figures as the President of Israel, would have to say about Martin Buber, internationally renowned for his presentation of Hasidic tales and his incorporation of aspects of Hasidic beliefs into existentialist patterns of thought.

In his response, the Rebbe turned to analogies, I now began to see, that would be more easily comprehended by me than those drawn from more recondite sources.

"The Buber versions of our Hasidic tales can be compared to reproductions of works of art. One gets a sense of what a great painting is like from a print, but one cannot apprehend the painting from the print any more than one can apprehend a great sculpture from a plaster copy. In terms of their value, it is true that some people are stirred by reproductions and copies to seek out the original and discover the secrets of its greatness. Most, however, are inclined to take simple satisfaction in the delusion that they have been given a painless revelation of artistic profundity. To the extent that Buber leads people to think that they are getting a genuine understanding of Hasidism without having to learn from the source, his influence is not constructive."

At this point I decided that I might safely inquire as to what the Lubavitcher Rebbe thought of the conduct of the Satmar Rebbe, Rabbi Joel Teitelbaum. I told the Rebbe that I asked Rabbi Teitelbaum, "If Israel exists as a state, would he find it preferable that Israel should not exist?"

"No, no," he replied rapidly and unhesitatingly, gesturing broadly with his pale hands as he spoke. I took his *no* to mean that Israel should not exist as a state, for he went on, in Yiddish, "I would say, *no*, I'd rather wait for the Messiah."

The Rebbe greets an individual from an Israeli delegation with President Shazar, 1966.

The Rebbe and the President of Israel Mr. Zalman Shazar, 1966.

Rabbi Schneerson leaned back and smiled at me, amused. As the shadow of his hat brim was removed, his face changed color, looking no longer ruddy but pallid, almost translucent. "Why should I comment," he asked good-humoredly, "about the relationship between a man in Williamsburg whom I do not know and the State of Israel, which I have never visited? It is one thing for me to discuss the Germans and the Jews—I am a Jew, and my own people have suffered and died at the hands of the Nazis. But this other question of yours really does not concern me."

THE REBBE INTERVIEWS

I forbore to press the point, particularly since we had already been talking for over half an hour, and I did not wish to encroach on his time or on that of those who were waiting patiently to see him. I thanked him for his courtesy and half-rose to leave, when he restrained me with a motion of his hand.

"Now that you have interviewed me, I'd like to interview you. Unless you have any objections?"

"Please," I said, "go right ahead."

"But I am afraid that I won't be as diplomatic with you as you have been with me." And the Rebbe grinned wickedly at me.

After a few questions about my background, he asked me about the subject matter of my books. When I protested that it was not easy to sum up in a sentence or two books that had taken me years to write, he retorted, "Surely I can expect a better summation from you than from anyone else."

He seemed particularly interested in my description of *On the Line*, a book in which I had attempted, by means of a series of fictional portraits of auto assembly workers, to demonstrate the impact of their work on their lives. It was a theme I had originally selected because it seemed to me, as a former factory worker, that it was being neglected by other novelists.

"What conclusions did you come to?"

The question nettled me. It struck me as obtuse, coming from a man of such subtle perception.

"Did you suggest," he persisted, "that the unhappy workers, the exploited workers, the workers chained to their machines, should revolt?"

"Of course not. It would have been unrealistic."

"What relation would you say that your book bears to the early work of Upton Sinclair?"

I was flabbergasted. Here I was, sitting in the study of a scholar of mystic lore late on a wintry night, and discussing not Chabad Hasidism, Aristotelianism or scholasticism, but proletarian literature! "Why," I said, "I would hope that it is less narrowly propagandistic than Sinclair's. I was trying to capture a mood of frustration

rather than one of revolution."

Suddenly I realized that he had led me to the answer that he was seeking—and what was more, with his next query I realized how many steps ahead of my faltering mind: "You could not conscientiously recommend revolution for your unhappy workers in a free country, or see it as a practical perspective for their leaders. Then how could one demand it from those who were being crushed and destroyed by the Nazis?"

"But when I questioned you, I wasn't associating myself with the Arendt position on Eichmann and the Jewish leaders," I protested. "I was simply trying to solicit your opinion of a question that has troubled me deeply."

"I realize that," the Rebbe smiled. "I am only suggesting that you might search for some of the answers in your own background and your own writing. After all, you have certain responsibilities which the ordinary man does not—your words affect not just your own family and friends, but thousands of readers."

"I'm not sure I know what those responsibilities are."

"First, there is the responsibility to understand the past. Earlier, you asked me about the future of Judaism. Supposing I ask you how you explain the past, the survival of Judaism over three millennia."

"Well," I said a bit uneasily, "the negative force of persecution has certainly driven people together who might otherwise disintegrate. I'm not certain that the disappearance of that persecution, whether through statehood in Israel or through the extension of democracy in this country, wouldn't weaken or destroy what you think of as Jewishness."

"Do you really think that only a negative force unites the little tailor in Melbourne and the Rothschild in Paris?"

"I wouldn't deny the positive aspects of Judaism."

Mr. Harvey Swados.

The Rebbe in conversation with a visitor in his office, 1971.

"Then suppose that scientific inquiry and historical research lead you to conclude that factors which you might regard as irrational have contributed to the continuity of Judaism. Wouldn't you feel logically bound to acknowledge the power of the irrational, even though you declined to embrace it?"

Hypnotized by the elegance with which he was leading me to meet him on his own grounds, I assented; as he continued, he turned occasionally to the metaphors of science, partly, I was sure, because they came to his mind as readily as the theological, and partly because he realized that I would find them intellectually more comfortable.

"The artist who wishes to present something more original than those copies of which we were speaking," once again he was making a connection between his responses to my questions and mine to his, "must bear in mind his responsibility not only to his readers but to his past, his heritage."

UTILIZE YOUR TALENTS

"You have a certain talent, a gift for expressing yourself so that thousands are swayed by what you write. Where does that talent come from?"

I was beginning to sweat. "Partly from hard work. From practice, from study."

"Naturally. But is it unscientific to suggest that you might owe some of it to your forebears? You are not self-created; you did not spring from nothing."

"I recognize," I said desperately, "that in the genes, the chromosomes…"

"If you wish. The point is, isn't it, that something has been transmitted to you by your father, your grandfather, your great-grandfather, down through the ages? And that you owe them a debt, a debt which you have the responsibility to try to repay?"

Now I was sweating heavily. In the silence that enveloped the room I could hear my watch ticking; my wife's hands, I noticed, were clenched as tightly as my own. But the Rebbe sat relaxed, seemingly with all the time in the world for me to fumble for responses. I had the feeling, like a student faking, that if I didn't say something, no matter what, I would be stuck here forever.

"Are you suggesting, Rebbe," I asked, "that I should re-examine my writing, or my personal code and my private lif?"

"Doesn't one relate to the other? Doesn't one imply the other?"

"That's a complicated question."

"Yes," he smiled amiably, "it certainly is." He paused. "I warned you that I wouldn't be diplomatic, didn't I?"

A MISSION

Silence again. Then I thanked him, as we all arose, for being so generous with his time. The Rebbe waved that aside. "We'll see," he said, "what your writing turns out like in the time ahead."

For a moment I thought he was referring to what I might write about our meeting; then I realized that few things could matter less to him. For he is a man quite without vanity, and what he was expressing was the hope that my work would go well – certainly better than before, which is always devoutly to be wished...

Outside, the snow was blowing furiously, piling up in swirling drifts along Eastern Parkway. Several Lubavitchers stood on the side with their wives, bundling up against the blast, but waiting nonetheless to hear our account of what the Rebbe had said to us.

The last thing in the world I wanted was to stand in the howling snow and summarize an hour and a half of intensely concentrated conversation, but they were so innocently eager that I had to try to give them some notion of what their leader had said to me—if not of my own reaction.

"Tell me," demanded one, beaming with pride at my recounting of the intellectual agility of Rabbi Schneerson, "what kind of impression did the Rebbe make on you? I know it is cold, but just tell me in one word."

There it was again. This time I did not bridle; perhaps the traditional good humor of the Hasidim as well as their bluntness had penetrated my chilled flesh at last. "If I had to choose one word to characterize him," I said, surprising myself more than my nodding listeners, "I guess I would choose the word 'kindly.'"

And my wife and I clambered into our snow-covered automobile for the long dangerous drive back home, both of us silent for a long time, wrapped in our own thoughts.

Mr. Harvey Swados was a journalist for the New York Times *and an acclaimed writer of historical novels. The above is from his unpublished papers in the collection of the University of Massachusetts, titled "I Am Interviewed by the Lubavitcher Rebbe" and "A Visit with the Satmar Rebbe." Several grammatical, stylistic and factual corrections were made.*

GLOSSARY

Ashkenazic. Jews from central and eastern European countries are called Ashkenazim, a term derived from the Hebrew word for Germany. Historically, Ashkenazic Jews spoke Yiddish, and their prayer services, customs and pronunciation of Hebrew are markedly different from those of Sephardic Jews.

Bar/Bat Mitzvah. The Jewish rite of passage into adulthood celebrated by a boy at age 13 and a girl at age 12. Literally "the son (or daughter) of the commandment," the celebration marks the beginning of the young person's official obligation to Jewish observance.

Chabad. An acronym for the Hebrew words *chochma*, *binah* and *daat*, "wisdom, understanding and knowledge." Chabad is a branch of the Chassidic movement (see below) that takes an intellectual approach to the service of G-d. In the second half of the 20th century, Chabad became known for bolstering Jewish life across the globe.

G-d. To indicate its holiness, the divine name is not written in its entirety, even in translation.

Chassidism; Chasid; Chasidic. From the Hebrew word *chesed*, "kindness," the Chasidic movement was founded in the 18th century by Rabbi Israel the son of Eliezer, later known as the Baal Shem Tov. Chasidic philosophy uses the mystical teachings of the Kabbalah to illuminate the deeper significance of Jewish prayer and ritual. The Chasid serves G-d with love and joy, recognizing the role of divine providence in every aspect of his or her life.

Lubavitch; Lubavitcher. Literally "the town of love," Lubavitch is the Yiddish name for the Russian village where the Chabad movement was based for over a century. The movement, its followers and leaders became known as "Lubavitch" or "Lubavitchers."

Mitzvah. Lit. "a commandment." Referring to Jewish observance, but the word is also used loosely for any good deed.

Rebbe. Literally "teacher," the term also refers to a Chassidic leader. In this book, "the Rebbe" is the seventh Chabad rebbe, Rabbi Menachem Mendel Schneerson (1902–1994).

Rebbetzin. The honorary title for the wife of a rabbi. In this book it refers to Rebbetzin Chaya Mushka Schneerson (1901–1988), the wife of the Rebbe (see above).

Sephardic. Jews from Spain and other Mediterranean countries are known as Sephardim. Their prayer services, customs and pronunciation of Hebrew differ from those of Ashkenazic Jews.

Shabbat. Day of rest. The Jewish Sabbath commemorates the completion of the six days of creation and G-d's resting on the seventh day. It is observed each week from sunset on Friday until nightfall on Saturday night with festive meals and special prayer services.

Simchat Torah. Literally "rejoicing with the Torah," the holiday that celebrates the completion of the yearly Torah-reading cycle. Simchat Torah is observed on the second day of the festival of Shemini Atzeret, which follows Sukkot (see below).

Sukkah; **Sukkot**. Sukkot is the eight-day festival which follows the high holy days of Rosh Hashanah and Yom Kippur. The *sukkah*, a small hut erected outdoors, commemorates the clouds that protected the Jews as they traveled through the desert from Egypt to the land of Israel. During the holiday, all meals and regular activities are conducted in the *sukkah*.

Tefillin. Black leather boxes containing parchment scrolls, tefillin are worn by men on the arm and the head during weekday morning prayers in fulfillment of the command, "You shall bind them as a sign upon your hand, and they shall be for you a reminder between your eyes" (Deuteronomy 6:8).

Torah. The Bible (Five Books of Moses); a teaching; the Torah scroll; used loosely for the general corpus of Jewish teachings.

Yeshivah. From the Hebrew word meaning "to sit," the term was traditionally used for schools where Talmud was studied. Today, any Jewish day school or Torah academy may be called a Yeshivah.

SOURCES

Adapted freely from the correspondence and conversations of the
Lubavitcher Rebbe. Below are the dates and sources
(note that several of the quotes are not published and
are therefore not sourced to any specific volume):

Page 3 **Action** Talk, December 12, 1964 (Likkutei Sichot, vol. 10, pp. 148ff). ¶ p. 7 **Anti-Semitism** Letter, October 23, 1991. ¶ p. 9 **Apology** Kfar Chabad Magazine, issue 862, p. 31.; letters, August 17, 1985, and September 1985. ¶ p. 11 **Birthdays** Talk, April 9, 1988 (Torat Menachem 5748, vol. 3, p. 158); talk, April 11, 1962 (Torat Menachem, vol. 33, pp. 283ff). ¶ p. 13 **Books** Talk, November 25, 1972 (Sichot Kodesh 5733, vol. 1, p. 201). ¶ p. 15 **Calling** Talk, September 24, 1956 (Torat Menachem, vol. 18, pp. 31ff). ¶ p. 17 **Caution** Talk, October 11th, 1970 (Kovetz Hitvaadut Shabbat Lech Lecha, 5777, pp. 12ff). ¶ p. 19 **Chabad House** Letter, March 9, 1969. ¶ p. 21 **Challenges** Talk, July 13th, 1954 (Torat Menachem, vol. 12, pp. 117ff). ¶ p. 25 **Charity** Letter, October 1973 (Igrot Kodesh, vol. 29, p. 11); letter, September 25, 1952 (Likkutei Sichot, vol. 2, p. 410). ¶ p. 27 **Charity Box** Talk, August 29, 1989 (Torat Menachem 5749, vol. 4, p. 215); talk, October 18, 1956 (Likkutei Sichot, vol. 29, p. 432). ¶ p. 29 **Childhood** Talk, October 8, 1988 (Sefer Hasichot 5749, vol. 1, p. 28). ¶ p. 31 **Clubs** Talk, September 29, 1980 (Sichot Kodesh 5741, vol. 1, pp. 177ff); letter, January 21, 1982. ¶ p. 33 **Conflict** Letter, April 18, 1962; talk, May 6, 1967 (Sichot Kodesh 5727, vol. 2, p. 107). ¶ p. 35 **Darkness** Talk, April 15, 1962 (Torat Menachem, vol. 33, p. 290). ¶ p. 37 **Days** Talk, July 13, 1954 (Torat Menachem, vol. 12, p. 116). ¶ p. 39 **Differences** Letter, March 14, 1987; letter, December 9, 1979 (Simpson-Chasdan commemorative booklet, 4 Tammuz 5768, p. 18; Shlichus Kehilchashah, p. 574). ¶ p. 43 **Drugs** Letter, December 11, 1964. ¶ p. 45

Education Letter, February 26, 1979. ¶ p. 47 **Elderly** Talk, July 28, 1980 (Sichot Kodesh 5740, vol. 3, pp. 883ff); talk, August 13, 1980 (ibid., pp. 972ff). ¶ p. 49 **Extrovert** Audience, October 1961; letter, July 8, 1965. ¶ p. 51 **Femininity** Talk, October 12, 1952 (Torat Menachem, vol. 7, pp. 116ff); talk, August 1, 1953 (Torat Menachem, vol. 9, p. 108). ¶ p. 53 **Food** Talk, June 14, 1958 (Torat Menachem, vol. 23, pp. 84ff). ¶ p. 55 **Gathering** Audience, June 17, 1951 (Torat Menachem, vol. 3, p. 162); letter, September 27, 1978; talk, December 13, 1986 (Torat Menachem 5747, vol. 1, p. 576). ¶ p. 57 **Harmony** Letter, April 14, 1981 (To Touch the Divine, p. 5); the Rebbe's foreword to Rabbi Shneur Zalman of Liadi: Biography, p. IX. ¶ p. 59 **Holidays** Letter, March 24, 1974 (Igrot Kodesh, vol. 29, p. 121). ¶ p. 63 **Humility** Letter, spring 1974 (Igrot Kodesh, vol. 29, p. 165); talks, summer 1982 (Likkutei Sichot, vol. 38, pp. 42ff). ¶ p. 65 **Illustrations** Letter, September 1982; response, June 1984. ¶ p. 67 **Intellect** Interview, March 7, 1960. ¶ p. 69 **Joy** Talk, September 23, 1987 (Torat Menachem 5747, vol. 4, p. 421); letter, 1976. ¶ p. 71 **Justice** Talk, August 7, 1985 (Torat Menachem 5745, vol. 5, p. 2722); letter, October 31, 1986. ¶ p. 73 **Kindness** Letter, September 1976 (Likkutei Sichot, vol. 14, p. 374); talk, March 23, 1978 (Likkutei Sichot, vol. 16, p. 625). ¶ p. 75 **Language** Letter, September 22, 1953 (Igrot Kodesh, vol. 8, p. 4). ¶ p. 77 **Leadership** Talk, January 17, 1951 (Torat Menachem, vol. 2, p. 213); talk, December 19, 1970 (Sichot Kodesh 5731, vol. 1, pp. 336ff). ¶ p. 81 **Light** Talk, October 12, 1974 (Sichot Kodesh 5735, vol. 1, p. 132); letter, November 25, 1977; see also talk, March 16, 1976 (Sichot Kodesh 5736, vol. 1, pp. 630ff). ¶ p. 83 **Livelihood** Talk, October 16, 1970 (Sichot Kodesh 5731, vol. 1, p. 73). ¶ p. 85 **Maimonides** Talk, April 20, 1987 (Torat Menachem 5744, vol. 3, p. 1546); talk, May 9, 1987 (ibid, pp. 1605ff). ¶ p. 87 **Matter** Letter, November 14, 1962; talk, May 24, 1986 (Torat Menachem 5746, vol. 3, p. 291). ¶ p. 89 **Mentor** Talk, August 9, 1986 (Torat Menachem 5746, vol. 4, pp. 173ff). ¶ p. 91 **Mergers** Letter, September 12, 1960 (Mr. Manchester, p. 61); letter, June 6, 1986. ¶ p. 93 **Mitzvah** Talk, June 2, 1967 (Sichot Kodesh 5727, vol. 2, p. 122); talk, March 25, 1983 (Torat Menachem 5743, vol. 3, p. 1210); talk, October 24, 1964 (Likkutei

Sichot, vol. 5, p. 91). ¶ p. 97 **Morality** Talk, April 1, 1983 (Torat Menachem 5743, vol. 3, p. 1298); talk, October 8, 1985 (Torat Men-achem 5746, vol. 1, pp. 405ff). ¶ p. 99 **Moshiach** Audience, winter 1972 (New York Times, March 27, 1972). ¶ p. 101 **Neighbors** Talk, April 10, 1969 (Likkutei Sichot, vol. 6, pp. 350ff; talk, April 10, 1969 (Sichot Kodesh 5729, vol. 2, pp. 68–9). ¶ p. 103 **Obstacles** Talk, April 16, 1965 (Torat Menachem, vol. 14, p. 64); talk, September 28, 1985 (Torat Menachem 5746, vol. 1, p. 145). ¶ p. 105 **Outreach** Audience, 1970s (Rabbi Israel Meir Lau, Out of the Depths, p. 202); audience, October 3, 1989. See also talk, October 7, 1985 (Likkutei Sichot, vol. 29, p. 367). ¶ p. 109 **Parents** Talk, October 13, 1990 (Likkutei Sichot, vol. 36, p. 95). ¶ p. 111 **Peace** Talk, May 13, 1990 (Sichos in English, vol. 44, p. 301); talks, February 8, 1975, January 30, 1976 and February 16, 1980 (Likkutei Sichot, vol. 29, pp. 125ff). ¶ p. 113 **Peer Pressure** Talk, August 30, 1954 (Torat Menachem, vol. 12, p. 190); audience, circa early 1950s. ¶ p. 115 **Prayer** Talk, September 30, 1982 (Torat Menachem 5743, vol. 1, p. 148ff); talk, September 18, 1969 (Likkutei Sichot, vol. 29, p. 186); see also talk, October 24, 1970. ¶ p. 117 **Prevention** Audience, November 26, 1968; letter, November 5, 1973. ¶ p. 119 **Pride** Letter, December 29, 1981 (Bronchtain commemorative booklet, 28 Kislev 5764, p. 18). ¶ p. 121 **Priorities** Talk, October 26, 1967 (Sichot Kodesh 5728, vol. 1, p. 96); talk, April 17, 1982 (Torat Menachem 5742, vol. 3, p. 1351). ¶ p. 123 **Prison** Letter, April 14, 1976 (Igrot Kodesh, vol. 31, p. 186). ¶ p. 125 **Protection** Letters, July 23 and August 25, 1958 (Katzman commemorative booklet, 22 Sivan 5759, pp. 6ff); May 25, 1974 (Likkutei Sichot, vol. 13, p. 211). ¶ p. 127 **Purpose** Talk, February 24, 1990 (Torat Menachem 5750, vol. 2, pp. 312ff). ¶ p. 129 **Racism** Letter, August 22, 1952 (Igrot Kodesh, vol. 6, p. 299); audience, September 1989. ¶ p. 131 **Rebuilding** Letter, April 26, 1965 (Igrot Kodesh, vol. 23, p. 374). ¶ p. 133 **Rebuke** Talk, October 23, 1965 (Likkutei Sichot vol. 10, pp. 24ff). ¶ p. 135 **Redemption** Talks, February 1, 1992 and July 6, 1991 (Shaarei Geulah, pp. 170ff). ¶ p. 139 **Repentance** Talk, September 25, 1952 (Likkutei Sichot, vol. 2, p. 409); Hitkashrut, no. 4, p. 11. ¶ p. 141 **Respect** Kfar Chabad Magazine, issue 862, p. 30. ¶ p. 143

Responsibility Letter, December 12, 1965 (Mondshine commemorative booklet, 17 Kislev 5768, p. 19); letter, April 1, 1966 (Igrot Kodesh, vol. 24, p. 110). ¶ p. 145 **Retirement** Talk, March 26, 1972 (Sichot Kodesh 5732, vol. 2, pp. 99ff). ¶ p. 149 **Self-Motivation** Letter, February 10, 1958 (Igrot Kodesh, vol. 16, p. 290); letter, January 20, 1957 (Igrot Kodesh, vol. 14, p. 360); letter, July 7, 1954 (Likutei Sipurei Hitvaaduyot, p. 603). ¶ p. 151 **Sight** Talk, October 27, 1983 (Torat Menachem 5744, vol. 1, pp. 487ff). ¶ p. 153 **Speech** Letter, February 21, 1977 (Igrot Kodesh, vol. 32, p. 130); talk, November 4, 1967 (Likkutei Sichot, vol. 5, pp. 44ff). ¶ p. 155 **Song** Talk, September 24, 1956 (Torat Menachem, vol. 18, p. 30); talk, October 3, 1961 (Torat Menachem, vol. 32, p. 112); talk, September 26, 1987 (Torat Menachem 5747, vol. 1, p. 92). ¶ p. 157 **Teaching** Talk, October 10, 1964 (Likkutei Sichot, vol. 5, p. 279); talk, September 18, 1976 (Sichot Kodesh 5736, vol. 2, p. 715). ¶ p. 159 **Technology** Talk, February 4, 1984 (Torat Menachem 5744, vol. 2, pp. 1040ff). ¶ p. 161 **Terror** Talk, May 16, 1956 (Likkutei Sichot, vol. 12, p. 258); letter, June 13, 1956 (Igrot Kodesh, vol. 13, p. 239). ¶ p. 163 **Unity** Talk, September 28, 1981 (Sichot Kodesh 5741, vol. 4, p. 764); letter, September 21, 1981 (Likkutei Sichot, vol. 24, pp. 583ff). ¶ p. 165 **Uplift** Talk, October 15, 1966 (Likkutei Sichot, vol. 5, pp. 46ff). ¶ p. 167 **Wealth** Audience, July 20, 1958 (Betzel Hachochmah, p. 16); talk, October 3, 1989 (Sichos in English, vol. 43, p. 19); talk, March 12, 1991 (Sichos in English, vol. 47, p. 219); talk, February 8, 1992 (Sefer Hasichot 5752, vol. 2, p. 390). ¶ p. 171 **Women** Talks, September 13, 1975 and April 10, 1976 (Likkutei Sichot, vol. 17, p. 146); talk, June 12, 1990 (Torat Menachem 5750, vol. 3, p. 345).

PHOTO CREDITS

Marc Asnin (pages 4, 13, 18, 22, 27, 43, 58, 70, 89, 98, 101, 103, 115, 134, 143 & 211)
Eliyahu Attar (p. 189 & 191), Bernard Mendoza (p. 136), Phillip Garvin (p. 177, 180 & 183), Chaim Baruch Halberstam (Chibah)/Algemeiner Journal (p. 130), Thomas McGovern (p. 106), Menachem Serraf (p. 8), Michel Setboun, Michele Studios/The Kahan Family (p. 195) and Dovid Zaklikowski (p. 85).

With photos from the archives of the Aleph Institute, Agudas Chasidei Chabad Library, Algemeiner Journal, Chabad of the West Coast, Federation of Jewish Communities of the CIS, Kehot Publications, Lubavitch House of London, National Committee for the Furtherance of Jewish Education, Menachem Wolf Collection, Tzach New York and Tzivos Hashem.

With appreciation to Rabbi Moshe Bogomilsky, Rabbi Yossi Butman, Yitzchak Yehudah Holtzman, Rabbi Chaim Nochum Cunin, Rabbi Mayer Harlig, Rabbi Yitzchok Kahan, Rabbi Nochem Kaplan, Yossel Mochkin, Ezzy Schaffran, Chana Sharfstein, Eli Slavin, Marco Swados and Rivkah Zaklikowski.

Some images were not marked with the photographer's name.
We regret any omissions.

ACKNOWLEDGEMENTS

First and foremost, I want to thank Rabbi Zushe Wilhelm, who spearheaded and partnered with us in the publishing of this book and guided it as the small building blocks slowly accumulated to form the finished product you are holding. May he and his wife have much nachas from their children and grandchildren.

The Advice for Life series was founded by Rabbi Simcha Zirkind, of blessed memory, who by the time he passed away had become to me a dear friend. May this book bring much spiritual pleasure to his soul on high. The original idea for this project came from Rabbi Mendel Chaiton.

Portions of the text were reviewed by Chana Silberg, Rabbi Mendel Lipskier and Rabbi Avraham Kievman. My thanks to Chana Sharfstein, who suggested the title, and, as always was generous with her suggestions and input.

Throughout the preparation, Rabbi Aaron Leib Raskin guided me, serving as a sounding board. He also reviewed the entire text, making many suggestions and corrections. My thanks also go to Alexander Heppenheimer and Rabbi Moshe Zaklikofsky for their final review.

I am grateful to Sarah Ogince, who tirelessly reviewed, commented on and clarified the material, and to Elana Rudnick and her dedicated team at Design Is Yummy for the fantastic design work.

Over the past few years, Shalom and Kayla Kramer have stood by my side, making this project possible. There are no words for your kindness. My thanks to Marc Asnin, a dear friend, who is always there to help; many of his photos grace these pages.

Above all, this project would not have been possible without my wife's patience and support through the many hours of late-night research and writing.

"Praise to G-d, for He is good, for His kindness is everlasting!"

Dovid Zaklikowski

In honor of the wedding
of our children
Moishe Begun and **Mashee Wilhelm**

לזכות החתן והכלה
משה ומאשי שיחיו בעגון
ליום נישואיהם, כ"ד סיון, ה'תשע"ז

Dedicated by Rabbi Zushe
and Esther Wilhelm

In loving memory of
Mrs. **Brana Shaina**

of blessed memory
Deitsch

לעילוי נשמת
מרת **בראנא שיינא** בת ר' **אברהם צבי** הלוי דייטש
נפטרה י"ג תשרי, ה'תשע"ה

In honor of our grandchildren
Motti, Meir, Shaina, Benny and **Mendel**
May their lives be filled with

joy and happiness

*Dedicated by Saba and Savta
Zaklikowski*

In honor of our children
Mendel and **Motti**

Dedicated by Itchy and Shaina
Glassner

KALEIDOSCOPE
UPLIFTING VIEWS ON DAILY LIFE

MORE IN THE SERIES
Advice for Life

Daily Life
Education
Marriage
From Life to Life

Dignified Differences A Special Soul
Learning on the Job Jewish Career Lessons

Hasidic Archives books are available in special discounts for bulk purchases in the United States
for corporations, institutions, and other organizations. For more information,
please contact us at RebbeAdvice@Gmail.com.